Revision
English

Revision English

New Edition

Ronald Forrest

Longman

Longman Group Limited,
Edinburgh Gate Harlow,
Essex CM20 2JE, England
and Associated Companies throughout the world.

First published 1968
Sixteenth impression 1996

Set in Garamond (Compugraphic)

Produced by Longman Singapore Publishers (Pte) Ltd
Printed in Singapore

ISBN 0-582-60981-X

Contents

2 Indirect Speech

3 Articles and Words of Quantity

4 Relatives

Acknowledgements

We are indebted to the following for permission to reproduce copyright material.

Heinemann Educational Books Limited, for extracts from *Weep Not Child* by James Ngugi; William Heinemann Limited, Publishers, for an extract from *Things Fall Apart* by Chinua Achebe; Routledge & Kegan Paul Limited, for an extract from *Child of Two Worlds* by Mugo Gatheru.

Preface

The purpose of this book is to provide material for revision of English towards the end of the secondary course. The actual year or years in which it is used will naturally vary from place to place.

Most teachers find that there is considerable need for remedial work at this level. By the second half of a secondary course most students are able to benefit from some knowledge of rules, but this benefit is very limited if the knowledge is not applied in numerous exercises. For this reason extensive practice has been provided. Some of the questions are of the objective type and these have been included to give teachers a quick and accurate means of assessing their students' progress. Although it is desirable that students should have practice in the type of question they are likely to encounter in examinations, this book is certainly not intended to be an 'examination book' in the traditional sense. Modern examinations require students to know the language rather than certain techniques, and it is the language this book aims to teach.

In continuous writing exercises and tests for learners of English as a second or foreign language, the provision of an outline helps the student to concentrate on correctness of language and relieves him of the search for ideas. I have tried to select topics for continuous writing and letter writing that are realistic and not remote from the students' experience.

It is too late in the last year or two of the secondary course to hope that students will pick up such an important part of the language as prepositions and phrasal verbs from reading. This is an area in which remedial work is absolutely essential. I have found that students rapidly improve their ability to handle these words if they do the type of exercise found in Section 7.

The Index is intentionally detailed. It is hoped that this will make it possible for the book to be used for reference purposes as well as in the classroom. A large number of verbs used in special patterns will be found in the Index.

The book is arranged according to topics and is not in course form. For revision work, which is inevitably·selective, most teachers prefer not to have a course with, for example, half a dozen varied topics contained in each chapter for a week's work. A book in which the material for revision is arranged according to topics can be more easily adapted to suit the needs of individual classes.

I should like to thank Mr. T. J. C. Baly for his most useful comments and corrections. The shortcomings which remain are my own.

Ronald Forrest

1 The Verb

Many verb mistakes are made because students use the forms of their own language. Like so much in language, using the correct verb form is largely a matter of habit. Knowing the rules is one thing; being able to apply them is another. Of course, the rules are worth knowing, and for this reason they are summarised in this chapter. Students who use the correct verb forms will not simply know the rules: they will have met so many examples that they almost instinctively use the correct forms. This ability will come not from merely knowing the rules but from wide and careful reading. It is therefore most important to consolidate your knowledge of verb forms by reading as much as possible. The various forms of the English verb are not easy to understand. This in itself is a good reason for not relying solely on rules. In language study it is only practice that makes perfect.

You will hardly need to be reminded that it is chiefly the tenses that cause difficulty. Do not confuse the word 'tense' with 'time'. Tense indicates sense rather than time. The tense we use depends on the sense we wish to give our sentence. For example, the Present Simple can be used to indicate the future:

He *leaves* for England next week.

In conditional sentences especially some of the tenses used have little connection with time:

If he *left* now, he would arrive before nine.

In this sentence the verb *left*, although it is the Past Simple of *to leave*, does not refer to a past event at all.

You will avoid a lot of tense mistakes if you remember that the tense does not always indicate the *time* of the action.

English tenses are not easy to understand. If they seem more complicated than the tenses in your own first language, you may comfort yourself with the thought that there are many languages with even more complicated tenses. There is an Australian language which has two future tenses for events which will happen today and three others for events happening from tomorrow onwards!

A The Tenses and the Passive

1 The Present Simple and Perfect Continuous Tenses

A common mistake is to use the Present Continuous when we should use the Present Simple. We use the Present Simple and *not* the Present Continuous for:

(a) *Facts*

A magnet *attracts* iron filings.

(b) *Repeated actions, customs and habits*

He *visits* his family every weekend.

Ethiopians *celebrate* Christmas on 7 January.

He *goes* to bed at eleven o'clock every night.

(c) *Abilities*

He *plays* the guitar very well.

(d) *The future*

(i) *after if in likely conditional clauses*

If he *comes* tomorrow, we shall remind him..

(ii) *after words like when, until, before, after, as soon as*

When the rain *stops*, we shall go out.

We can't begin until he *arrives*.

They will stop playing as soon as the whistle *blows*.

In the above four cases the Present Continuous cannot be used in place of the Present Simple.

Do not make the mistake of trying to use a Present form of the Past Habitual:

He *used to get up* at five o'clock.

To show present habit we simply use the Present Simple (as in (b) above):

He *gets up* at five o'clock.

There is, however, a pattern in which *used to* can occur in both the Past and the Present tenses:

He *was used to getting up* at five o'clock.

He *is used to getting up* at five o'clock.

By using the verb *to be* before *used to* we imply more than habit. *To be used to doing something* means *to be so accustomed to doing something that it is no longer difficult.*

EXERCISE 1

Write ten sentences using the Present Simple to indicate facts.

EXERCISE 2

Write ten sentences using the Present Simple to indicate repeated actions.

EXERCISE 3
Write five sentences using the Present Simple to indicate customs and five to indicate habits.

EXERCISE 4
Write ten sentences using the Present Simple to indicate abilities.

EXERCISE 5
a Write five sentences using the Present Simple to indicate the Future after *if* in likely conditional clauses.
b Write five sentences using the Present Simple to indicate the Future after *when, until, as soon as, after, before*.

The Present Simple and Continuous for Future Plans

For an event which has been definitely planned for the future we can use either the Present Simple or the Present Continuous instead of the Future:

He *takes* the examination next week.

He *is taking* the examination next week.

She *leaves* school in June.

She *is leaving* school in June.

The Present Simple used in this way implies that the event will take place according to a programme, timetable or calendar, while the Present Continuous here carries the idea of an intention.

EXERCISE 6
a Write a paragraph of five sentences (using five different verbs in the Present Simple) about the plans of a person who is going to fly round the world.
b Write five sentences (using five different verbs in the Present Continuous) about the future plans of members of your class and family.

The Present Continuous with 'Always'

We normally use the Present Simple for habits, but if we include in the sentence a word like *always, continually, constantly*, we can use the Present Continuous. This is more forceful than the Present Simple and normally implies that the speaker or writer does not approve of the action of the subject of the sentence.

He *is always asking* for loans.

She *is always talking*.

He *is continually making* a nuisance of himself.

EXERCISE 7
Write ten sentences using the Present Continuous with *always, continually* or *constantly* to show disapproval.

The Present Continuous for Temporary Activities

The Present Continuous, like all the Continuous Tenses, indicates an activity which is temporary. It describes something happening now, but not necessarily at this very moment. For example, we could say

> The headmaster is writing a book

when we know that at this moment he is interviewing students.

EXERCISE 8

Change the infinitives in brackets to either the Present Simple or the Present Continuous tense:

1 He (speak) five languages quite fluently.
2 He now (learn) Russian.
3 The moon (go) round the earth.
4 He (listen) to the radio, so don't disturb him.
5 He always (complain) about his health.
6 My brother (write) a letter and I (read) a book.
7 He usually (drive) very carefully, but today he (drive) recklessly.
8 We (be used) to living on a small income.
9 The term always (end) on a Friday.
10 The O.A.U. usually (meet) in Addis Ababa.

2 Verbs Rarely Found in Continuous Forms

There are certain verbs which are rarely found in the Continuous forms. For example, early in our study of English we realise (even if we do not learn the rule) that the verb *to be* is used in the Present Simple whether we are talking about something which is going on now or something which is habitual:

> I *am* late now.

> I *am* often late.

We can therefore say that *to be* is a verb not usually found in the Continuous form (except, of course, in the passive).

There are several verbs of this kind. They describe states or feelings which are thought to continue indefinitely. It is advisable to acquaint oneself thoroughly with these verbs. They are more easily remembered if we think of them as falling into six groups:

1. Verbs for states over which we have no control

see   I see that it is raining again.

(Compare *look*, e.g. *He is looking at a map*. Seeing is a state over which we have no control once we have our eyes open, but we can choose to look or not look.)

It is only when the verb *see* describes what happens to us when we have our eyes open that it is not used in the continuous forms. It can have several other meanings and for these the continuous forms can be used:

The manager *is seeing* the applicants. (interviewing)

The tourists *are seeing* the ancient monuments this morning. (touring)

hear   I *hear* the rain falling.   *Listen* is used about a voluntary action, e.g. *I am listening to the radio*.)

feel (when intransitive)	This blanket *feels* very damp.
taste (when intransitive)	This meat *tastes* good.
smell (when intransitive)	His breath *smells* bad.

2. *Verbs for ideas*

know	He now *knows* as much about the subject as you do.
understand	We *understand* what he is talking about.
think (that)	I *think* (*that*) it is time for us to leave. (Compare *think of*, e.g. *He is thinking of his future*.)
believe	I *believe* what he is saying is true.
disbelieve	She *disbelieves* her own father.
suppose	I *suppose* you are right.
doubt	I *doubt* if he will succeed.
agree	We *agree* with his suggestion.
disagree	We *disagree* with his point of view.
realise	They *realise* they cannot win the game.
imagine	I *imagine* you will succeed.
consider (that)	His teacher *considers* him a good student. (Compare *consider* when it means *think over*, e.g. *He is still considering what action he should take*.)
notice	I *notice* that you have been promoted.
recognise	Britain now *recognises* the new regime.
forget	I *forget* his name.
remember	I *remember* what he said.
recall	I *recall* the actual words of the speaker.

3. *Verbs for liking and disliking*

like	I *like* the book I am reading.
dislike	I *dislike* this painting.
love	He *loves* his children.
hate	He *hates* flattery.
detest	She *detests* people who are unkind to animals.
despise	He *despises* this man because he is a coward.
prefer	We *prefer* to go without him.
forgive	I *forgive* you for the unpleasant things you have said.

trust	I *trust* you do not object.
distrust	I *distrust* this man.

4. *Verbs for wishing*

wish	He *wishes* to leave as early as possible.
want	They *want* more than they are entitled to.
desire	The Company *desires* to recruit a branch manager.

5. *Verbs for possession*

possess	He *possesses* well over a thousand books.
have	He *has* more money than he needs. (The rule applies only when *have* means *possess*. In other cases the Continuous can be used, e.g. *We are now having lunch*.)
own	His father *owns* several acres of land.
belong to	This book *belongs to* John Brown.

6. *Certain other verbs*

be	He *is* very patient. (The Continuous can be used if we wish to describe a state which is only temporary. For example, we can say: He *is* not *being* very patient over this matter. The Simple is used to describe a characteristic that is thought of as being permanent.)
appear	She *appears* to be more intelligent than she is. (Only when *appear* means *seem*. When it means *come into view*, the Continuous is possible, e.g. *Leaves are now appearing on the trees*.)
seem	This *seems* to be the book I should read.
mean	He doesn't know what you *mean*.
please	(usually in passive) He *is pleased* with the news.
displease	(usually in passive) We *are displeased* with her.
differ	The two brothers *differ* in many respects.
matter	His opinion *matters* to me.
depend	His future now *depends* on the decision of the judge.
resemble	He *resembles* his father.
deserve	He *deserves* the medal.
refuse	He *refuses* to take part in our game.
result	His failure *results* from his laziness.
suffice	What we have *suffices*.
consist of	The course *consists* of twenty lessons.
contain	The tin *contains* an ounce of tobacco.
hold	This torch *holds* two batteries. (Only when *hold* means *contain*.)
fit	Now that it has been altered this jacket *fits* him.
suit	The blue dress she is wearing *suits* her.

The previous verbs are occasionally found in the Continuous forms. This is especially true in colloquial English. If the word 'always' (or a word of similar meaning) is used to imply frequent repetition which meets with the disapproval of the speaker (as in the examples on page 3), a Continuous tense can be used with some of the above verbs.

He is always forgetting his books.

He is always foreseeing disaster.

With this exception, it is generally advisable for a student at this level to avoid using the above verbs in Continuous forms.

EXERCISE 9

Change the infinitives in brackets to either the Present Simple or the Present Continuous tense:

1 Now we (know) more about the use of the Continuous tenses.
2 They no longer (resemble) each other.
3 The bicycle which he (use) today (belong) to me.
4 Now that it is too late he (want) to go to the cinema.
5 I (doubt) if he will come.
6 You (understand) what he is talking about?
7 That student (deserve) a prize he has worked so hard.
8 What he (mean) is not clear to me.
9 They (work) hard when they (have) to.
10 I (not remember) his name, but I (think) my brother will be able to tell you.
11 The exercise we (do) now (appear) to be easy but it (contain) some tricky sentences.
12 Now that you have given me an example I (see) what you (mean).
13 This room (smell) very stuffy this morning.
14 His future (matter) very much not only to himself but also to his family.
15 The ice-cream we are eating (taste) very good.
16 I (know) now that he (understand) what I (mean).
17 Our landlord now (own) five houses.
18 He still (consider) what should be done.
19 The doctor (feel) the patient's pulse at this moment.
20 He (love) his children and (prefer) to spend money on school fees rather than on himself.
21 Oladele and Segun (not agree) about how they should share the reward.
22 He now (realise) he has made a mistake and (think) of resigning.
23 He always (doubt) my word and this makes me angry.
24 We (add) another room to our house which already (consist of) seven rooms.
25 Although the event happened thirty years ago, he still (recall) it clearly.
26 His opinion (not matter).

27 The letter which I (read) (appear) to have been written by an educated person.

28 He now (feel) that there is little hope of success.

29 Today the average schoolboy (know) more about science than most scientists did two hundred years ago.

30 I (believe) that he (think) of his failure in the examination and that is why he (have) such a miserable expression on his face.

3 Present Perfect and Present Perfect Continuous Tenses

The Present Perfect

This tense gives considerable difficulty because students look upon it as a Past rather than a Present tense. *It is a Present tense.* It describes events which happened in the past but are closely connected with the present. If we bear this important point in mind we will avoid many tense mistakes. It is a very common mistake to confuse the Present Perfect and the Past Simple tenses.

A person arrives at an airport and says, "I have lost my ticket." He would not say "I lost my ticket." Losing his ticket has a very definite effect on the present for the would-be passenger and the result will probably be that he will be delayed.

Later, however, when he reaches his destination, he would say to his friends, "I lost my ticket, but eventually I got another one and made the journey." Now he sees the loss of his ticket as a past event not closely connected with the present, and he therefore uses the Past Simple.

In many cases which tense we should use is decided for us by the presence in the sentence of an adverb of past time. No matter how closely connected with the present an event may be, the moment we use an adverb of past time we are obliged to use a past tense.

I saw him *last week*.

We first met *in 1981*.

(An adverb of past time which covers a period of time up to the present requires the Present Perfect tense:

He has been here *since 1981*.

She has been a nurse *for five years*.)

Even if the adverb of past time refers to only a very short while ago we must use a past tense

Mr. Ikejiani came into the room *a minute ago*.

The plane touched down *ten seconds ago*.

In the first sentence we are not implying by our use of the Past Simple that Mr. Ikejiani is no longer in the room; nor in the second sentence are we implying that the plane is no longer at this airport. We use the Past Simple because the adverbs of past time require it.

Some adverbs can be of either past or present time according to when they are used. For example, if we use the adverb *this morning* at 10 a.m., it is an adverb of present time, whereas at 2 p.m. it is an adverb of past time. Our tenses change accordingly:

(Spoken at 10 a.m.) I have seen the Principal this morning.

(Spoken at 2 p.m.) I saw the Principal this morning.

Notice that an adverb of past time may sometimes consist of several words:

I saw the Empire State Building *when I was in New York*. *When I was in New York* is an adverb of past time; it could be replaced by a date – *in 1981*.

There are certain adverbs associated with the Present Perfect rather than with the Past Simple. When we use such words as *lately*, *recently*, *just*, *already*, we show that the past event is closely connected with the present and we therefore use the Present Perfect tense.

We have not been to the cinema *lately*.

He has *recently* got married.

The results have *just been announced*.

He has *already* announced his decision.

There is another useful guide to which tense we should use. Any word or group of words indicating a period of time beginning in the past and continuing up to the present necessitates the use of the Present Perfect tense. Some adverbs of this kind are: *up to the present*, *yet*, *not yet*, *ever*, *never*.

Up to the present we have had no news of the escaped prisoner.

Have you read that book *yet*?

I have *not yet* read that book.

Have you *ever* been to Paris?

I have *never* been to Paris.

We often think of the whole lifetime of a person when we ask a question such as:

Have you been to Paris? (with *ever* understood)

This question implies that the person still has a chance of going to Paris. If we know, however, that he has no chance or intention of going to Paris, or if we are thinking of a specific trip he made to Europe, we would say:

Did you go to Paris?

In this case we use the Past Simple because an adverb of past time is understood.

The words *since* and *for* are frequently used in a phrase describing a period of time beginning in the past and continuing up to the present. When they are used in this way the Present Perfect tense is required:

He has lived in this house *since he came to our town*.

He has been a teacher *for twenty years*.

For can, of course, be used with the Past Simple. In this case the period of time it precedes began *and ended* in the past whereas in the above example with the Present Perfect the period began in the past but has continued right up to the present. Compare:

He *was* a teacher *for twenty years*. (1961–1981)

EXERCISE 10

Change the infinitives in brackets to either the Present Perfect or the Past Simple tense:

1 During this year we (see) many advances in computer technology.
2 He (stop) digging when he was told that the treasure had already been found.
3 He (run) away to sea when he was a boy and he is still a sailor.
4 Up to now he (be rejected) by every employer he has applied to.
5 Europeans (live) in Australia since the eighteenth century.
6 Her family first (go) to live in Abeokuta thirty years ago.
7 Our headmaster (be born) in 1930.
8 I just (join) the library so that I can spend every evening studying there.
9 The author who is lecturing tonight (write) over twenty novels.
10 I (be) very glad to receive your letter.
11 Last year John (win) a prize for composition. He (win) several prizes since he (come) to this school.
12 I just (read) the book which I (borrowed) from the library a week ago.
13 Tobacco (be brought) from America in the sixteenth century and (be smoked) all over the world in the last four hundred years.
14 Since 1900 science (progress) rapidly.
15 His grandfather, who just (die), (be married) three times.
16 Up till now she (make) a good impression on her teachers.
17 He (be ill) last month but he (recover) now.
18 She often (go) to Ibadan when she (be) a student at Ife.
19 We (not yet finish) this exercise.
20 I never (know) my late grandmother to lose her temper.
21 I (see) the editor last Friday but I not (see) him since then.
22 She (be) a nurse from 1975–8 but since then she not (work).
23 This book first (appear) in 1978.
24 His sister (get) married in 1978 and (have) three children so far.
25 Our history teacher (read) every available book on the history of Zimbabwe and can be said to be an authority on the subject.
26 My father (work) as a carpenter since the day he (leave) school and isn't a rich man.
27 He often (work) until midnight when he (be) a student.
28 Before he (join) our club he (play) football for his school team.
29 I can phone you now as I (have) a telephone installed.
30 Since the day he (fall) ill he (do) a lot of reading.

31 I now (read) your letter and will do my best to help you.
32 We (own) this house since 1975.
33 Ten years ago I (go) to New York but I not (go) there since.
34 I (learn) to ride a horse when I (be) very small.
35 He just (return) from England.
36 I (meet) him when he (be) still a student.
37 She first (take) the examination three years ago and (take) it twice since then.
38 I (have) my hair cut three times last term but I (have) already cut it twice this term.
39 I nearly (finish) this exercise on the Past Simple and Present Perfect.
40 Our Maths teacher (give) us a lot of work last week but he not (give) us very much so far this week.

The Present Perfect Continuous

Like the Present Perfect Simple, which we have just revised, this tense indicates a past event closely connected with the present. It is distinguished from the Present Perfect Simple in that it is used in three special ways:
1. To indicate an activity or state which started in the past has gone on until the present.

  We *have been revising* verbs for three weeks.

  He *has been washing* the windows since ten o'clock.
2. To *emphasise* that a past activity or state, connected with the present but now ended, has been continuous or repeated.

  We *have been playing* all the afternoon.

  I *have been taking medicine* for my cold since Thursday.
3. To indicate that a past activity or state, connected with the present but now ended, has an important result which is now being experienced. This is not an easy use of the Present Perfect Continuous to understand and you should study these six examples carefully:

  The workmen *have been digging up* the road, and now the traffic cannot pass.

  We *have been driving* along muddy roads, and now the car is dirty.

  He *has been training* for several weeks and should do very well in the cross-country race.

  He *has been drinking* and can't walk straight.

  I *have been working* in the garden and need a bath.

  He *has been studying* all night and has fallen asleep in class.

In each of the above sentences there is the idea *'and this is the result'*. For this reason we use the Continuous rather than the Simple form of the Present Perfect.

Remember that there are certain verbs which are rarely found in the Continuous forms (pp. 4–8).

Change the infinitives in brackets to either the Present Perfect Simple or the Present Perfect Continuous.

1 Now that I (finish) *Oliver Twist* I shall read *A Tale of Two Cities*.
2 Our teacher (talk) about tenses for over an hour, and we wish he would stop.
3 Usman (fast) since sunrise and he is not allowed to eat until sunset.
4 We (be) students in this school for the last five years.
5 He (talk) for three hours and soon he will have to stop.
6 The workmen (build) our new classrooms since last May.
7 My brother recently (enter) the university.
8 He (bargain) with the trader for fifteen minutes and they (not agree) yet on a price.
9 My teacher (correct) books for two hours and (not finish) yet.
10 I (understand) everything you (say) for the last twenty minutes.
11 His father (smoke) cigarettes for twenty years and now (be advised) by his doctor to stop.
12 He (not visit) us since 1981.
13 I (wait) for him since half past eight and I shall wait only another five minutes.
14 He (revise) for the history examination for several weeks and I believe he will do well.
15 The Prime Minister just (announce) that the treaty (be signed).
16 A strong wind (blow) all the afternoon.
17 Mr. Okeke (try) to start his car for the last twenty minutes and is beginning to despair.
18 He already (write) a letter to his father.
19 I (save up) to buy a camera since last September but I don't expect to have enough money for another two months.
20 We (do) a tense exercise for the last few minutes.

4 The Past Simple and Past Continuous Tenses

These two tenses are so often confused that it is a good idea to revise them together and see how they differ.

Remember that if the past activity or state is closely connected with the present, we use the Present Perfect tenses.

For past activities and states which are not connected with the present we use either the Past Simple or the Past Continuous (with the exception of those requiring the Past Perfect discussed on pp. 15–16).

Most students make the mistake of using the Past Continuous far too often. We use the Past Simple unless:

1. An activity was going on when another one took place:

   He *was reading* a newspaper when I entered the room.

   I *was listening* to the radio when the phone rang.

   The second activity could be replaced by a point in time:

   He was reading a newspaper *at eight o'clock.*

   I was listening to the radio *at half past nine.*

2. We wish *to emphasise* that two actions were taking place at the same time:

   I *was reading* while my sister *was writing.*

   The students in the next class *were making* a noise while we *were taking* our biology examination.

3. We wish *to emphasise* that an activity was continuous over a certain period (often with an expression like *all day, all the morning*).

   I *was·working* hard all last week.

   The gardener *was cutting* the grass all yesterday afternoon.

4. We wish to show disapproval, using a word like *always*:

   She *was always making* a disturbance in the classroom.

   He *was always asking* for favours.

(See note on Present Continuous used in this way on p. 7.)

BEWARE of using the Past Continuous in any other circumstances.

Whenever you think of using the Past Continuous, ask yourself the questions: "Is it important to the sense that this activity went on continuously? Even if the activity did go on for a long time, is this fact important to the sense?" And do not forget that there are certain verbs rarely found in the Continuous forms (see pp. 4–8.)

A common and serious mistake is to use the Past Continuous for repeated or habitual activities in the past. We must use the Past Simple:

   Last year we *went* to the cinema every Saturday.

   She often *took part in* dramatic productions when she was at school.

   He frequently *borrowed* books from the school library.

Repeated or habitual activities in the past can also be expressed by *used to* + *infinitive:*

   We *used to write* a composition every week.

   He *used to play* football when he was at school.

(There is no Present form of *used to*. See p. 2.)

EXERCISE 12

Change the infinitives in brackets to either the Past Simple or the Past Continuous tense:

1 He (spend) three years in France when he (be) a young man.

2 We (do) a lot of oral work in Form Two.

3 She (live) with her parents when the war (break) out.

4 Our school football team (win) the championship last year.

5 He (read) a newspaper when I (see) him.

6 His great grandfather (be born) a hundred years ago.
7 My sister (cook) a meal for our ten guests all the afternoon.
8 He (walk) down to the beach, (take) off his clothes, (put on) swimming trunks and (spend) an hour in the water.
9 What (do) you do at eight o'clock yesterday evening? I (play) table-tennis.
10 The night watchman (sleep) when I (call) at your house.
11 We (play) football when the ball (be kicked) through a window.
12 As we (climb) the mountain, our guide (slip) and (fall).
13 He (read) a lot of poetry when he (be) a student.
14 All last week he (paint) his house.
15 In the middle ages many people (die) in famines.
16 While it still (rain), we (leave) the meeting and (cycle) home.
17 We (play) cards in the living-room while thieves (take) our possessions from the bedroom.
18 That house (be worth) half its present value when I (buy) it.
19 I (spend) a lot of money on books yesterday afternoon.
20 I (sit) in my own room when I (hear) the dog bark.
21 I (cycle) along the road when I suddenly (see) an elephant.
22 The little girls (be) afraid because it (get) dark.
23 The teacher (come) into the library to see what we (do).
24 While I (learn) French, I often (confuse) the tenses.
25 Papers and books (be) scattered everywhere in his study. Obviously Mr. Ajose (write) a book.
26 The patient (recover) from his illness by the time the drugs (arrive). He (leave) hospital a week later.
27 He (do) as he was told as soon as I (remind) him of the headmaster's threat.
28 While he (dig) in the garden, he (find) an old coin.
29 When he first (meet) her, she (work) as a typist.
30 I (be) glad to travel with you as my car (give) trouble.

EXERCISE 13
Change the infinitives in brackets to either the Past Simple or the Past Continuous tense:

Yesterday morning when I (leave) my home to go shopping, the sun (shine). It (be) so pleasant that I (decide) to walk to the market instead of taking a bus. On my way I (see) an old friend of mine on the other side of the road, and I (call) to him. He (go) in the opposite direction towards a crowd of people at a bus-stop and (not hear) me. I (cross) the road to speak to him but I (be) too late as he (be) already on the bus. I (think) that I might not have an opportunity to meet him again for several years as I (know) he (go) to the United States to study. Later that morning I (talk) to a shopkeeper when my friend (come) into the shop. We (spend) the rest of the morning together chatting about old times.

EXERCISE 14

Change the infinitives in brackets to either the Past Simple or the Past Continuous tense:

The debate (begin) at five o'clock while some of the students still (arrive). The chairman (say) he (think) everybody should make an effort to arrive on time. He (read) out the motion for debate: 'Rats are found only in dirty houses', and then (introduce) the main speakers. The proposer (speak) for twenty minutes. The opposer (treat) the subject humorously and the applause for his speech (last) over a minute. Several people (speak) from the floor, but because of a time limit of three minutes for each speech some speakers (have) to stop while they still (develop) their arguments. As the proposer (make) his closing remarks, somebody (release) a rat which (run) in front of the main speakers. Since nobody (want) to admit that this was a dirty house, not one vote (be cast) for the motion.

5 The Past Perfect and Past Perfect Continuous Tenses

The Past Perfect

This tense is best understood if it is called the 'before' tense. When we wish to indicate that an event happened *before* another event in the past, we use the Past Perfect. Like the Past Continuous this tense is used far too often by some students. It is not often that we wish to convey the idea of one event happening before another, and for this reason we do not use this tense frequently. Sometimes it is clear that one event occurred before the other without using the Past Perfect. Study the following sentences:

The lesson *had begun* when we arrived.

The lesson *began* before we arrived.

In the first sentence the Past Perfect is necessary to make it clear that the order of events was:

    1. The beginning of the lesson,

    2. Our arrival.

The lesson *began* when we arrived would give a different meaning — that the beginning of the lesson and our arrival occurred at the same time. In the second sentence the use of the word *before* makes the order quite clear, and the Past Perfect tense is unnecessary.

The Past Perfect is used with a point of time in the past to show that the event occurred before that point:

By two o'clock he *had read* most of the novel.

In 1982 he *had been employed* as a clerk for ten years.
(The Past Perfect is also used in rejected conditions (see p. 22) and for unfulfilled wishes in the past (see p. 54).)

The Past Perfect Continuous

This is a comparatively unimportant tense. It is used when we wish to indicate that an event happened before another event in the past and that the event was continuous (or was still continuing at a certain point in the past).

We *had been waiting* for half an hour when the other team arrived.

He *had been working* for that company for ten years when he was promoted.

In 1978 he *had been studying* in Ibadan for two years.

At five o'clock we *had been playing* tennis for an hour.

EXERCISE 15

Change the infinitives in brackets to the Past Perfect, Past Simple or the Past Perfect Continuous Tense:

1 He (forget) my name, so I reminded him.
2 I (discuss) the matter with my headmaster before I (write) to my father.
3 After he (finish) his studies he (live) in England for two years.
4 By ten o'clock the band (play) for three hours.
5 Although I (ask) her to lend me the book, she (leave) it at home.
6 He (say) that the window (be broken) while he was on holiday.
7 I (not visit) England for seven years when I (go) there last year.
8 My English teacher (give) me a good report last term.
9 We (live) in Lagos for twenty years when we (decide) to go to Port Harcourt.
10 The artist (finish) the painting at exactly three o'clock.
11 The fire already (destroy) much of the building when the firemen (arrive)).
12 She (study) French for two years when she (go) to Paris.
13 He (tell) me he (read) the history notes dictated by our teacher.
14 In 1983 the United Nations (be established) thirty-seven years.
15 When the war (break out), Mr. Bello (work) as a teacher for seventeen years.
16 He (take) two degrees before he (become) a teacher.
17 It (be rumoured) that a Member of Parliament (be shot).
18 When I (go) to see the doctor at five o'clock, I (suffer) from stomach-ache for several hours.
19 The water (boil) for ten minutes when the cook (pour) it on the tea.
20 He (be warned) on several occasions and the headmaster now (have) no alternative but to expel him.
21 The shop (sell) all the bread by the time I (get) there.

22 She (qualify) as a nurse and then (get) married.

23 It (rain) for three hours, but we (decide) we had to set out.

24 The little girl (cry) because somebody (take) her chocolate.

25 When I (arrive) at the bus-stop, I (learn) that the bus already (leave).

26 He (find) the lecture easy to follow because he (read) about the subject.

27 I (swim) for over half an hour when the sea suddenly (become) rough.

28 I (wear) that jacket for a year when somebody (steal) it.

29 As he recently (visit) his parents, he (not want) to write to them immediately.

30 She (cook) the meal for over an hour when we (arrive) at the house.

6 The Future and Future Continuous Tenses

The Future Simple and 'going to'

The difficulty with the Future Simple is not so much the difference between *will* and *shall* as when to use special forms such as *going to*.

Firstly, you should note that in modern English the distinction between *will* and *shall* for the Pure Future has almost disappeared. We can use *will* for any person when we simply want to indicate that an event will happen in the future. Strictly speaking, *will* used with the first person indicates a promise or intention. In practice there is no difference between the borrower who says

I *shall* return your money tomorrow.

and the one who says

I *will* return your money tomorrow.

Only a rigid grammarian would prefer to believe the borrower who uses *will*!

The future can be expressed by *going to* + *infinitive* if there is the idea of intention, certainty or prediction.

We *are going* to have dinner at eight o'clock.

She *is going to* leave school in June.

This house *is going to* fall down.

It is, of course, quite correct to use *will* in place of *going to*.

The *going to* construction is particularly common to express decisions that we have already taken:

We *are going to spend* August in Kano.

But it is not used for a future action decided at the moment of speaking:

I'm hungry. I think *I'll cook* a meal.

Usually it does not occur in conditions:

If you tell him the truth, *he'll be disappointed*.

Complete the following sentences, using *going to* wherever possible and *will* or *shall* in other cases:

1 It is very cloudy and I'm sure it ... rain.
2 He ... leave for England on Thursday.
3 I ... stay in this town for a month.
4 This train ... take you to Lagos.
5 He ... give you change if you ask him.
6 I ... read a book tonight.
7 He ... clean his bicycle this evening.
8 The sun ... rise at half past five tomorrow morning.
9 The headmaster ... punish that boy if he is late again.
10 When ... you telephone your father?
11 Tomorrow ... be the last day of the month.
12 His wife ... have a baby next month.
13 I don't know if you ... be chosen for the play.
14 Those trees ... be cut down next week.
15 The gardener ... water the lawn if we tell him to.
16 We ... have more students in this school next term.
17 Our dog ... bark if someone tries to break into the house.
18 The train ... arrive in ten minutes' time.
19 The President ... make an important speech tonight.
20 If you spend a few months in Italy, you ... become quite fluent in Italian.

The Future Continuous

This tense is used for an activity or a state which begins before and continues after a point of future time:

He *will be flying* across the Sahara at two o'clock tomorrow afternoon. Here the Future Simple would not be a suitable tense because the flight will obviously last longer than an instant; it will begin before and continue after two o'clock. Consider these further examples:

We *shall be playing* football at half past four tomorrow.

When he arrives, they *will be waiting* at the railway station for him.

Next Tuesday we *shall be taking* our final examinations.

The Future Continuous can also be used to indicate that an activity or state will be going on over a period of future time:

I *shall be working* in the library all tomorrow morning.

My brother *will be studying* at the university next year.

Our teacher *will be correcting* examination papers all next week.

In such cases as the above three the Future Continuous is used for emphasis and it would not be grammatically wrong to use the Future Simple.

The Future Continuous can be used instead of the Present Continuous to show that an event has been definitely planned for the future:

She *will be leaving* school in June.

(See p. 3 for a note on the use of the Present Continuous in this way.)

EXERCISE 17
Write five sentences using the Future Continuous to indicate an activity or state beginning before and continuing after a point of future time.

EXERCISE 18
Write five sentences using the Future Continuous to emphasise that an activity or state will be going on continuously over a period of future time.

EXERCISE 19
Write five sentences using the Future Continuous to indicate that an event has been definitely planned for the future.

7 Other Uses of 'shall' and 'will'

Apart from helping to form the Future tense these verbs have other uses.

If *shall* is used with the second or third persons it implies a promise or a threat:

You *shall* have what you deserve.

He *shall* not go to the cinema until he finishes his work.

Shall is used in questions about the wish or suggestions of another person:

Shall I help you with your work? (= Do you wish me to help you with your work?)

Shall we have a game of table-tennis? (= Do you wish to have a game of table-tennis?)

What *shall* I do next? (What do you suggest I do next?)

Will can express willingness or a wish, especially in questions:

Will you let me have the book as soon as possible?

If you *will* let me have your address, I shall send you our magazine regularly.

Will not can therefore have the meaning *refuses*:

He *will not* tell me his name.

Will can also imply insistence:

He has been told several times that unripe bananas are bad for him but he *will* eat them.

Will can be used for characteristics:

Water *will* freeze at 0 °C.

EXERCISE 20
Write five sentences using *shall* with the second or third persons to imply a promise or a threat.

EXERCISE 21

Write five sentences using *shall* in questions about the wish or suggestion of another person.

EXERCISE 22

Write five sentences using *will* to express willingness or a wish.

EXERCISE 23

Write five sentences using *will* to express insistence.

EXERCISE 24

Write five sentences using *will* to express characteristics.

8 The Future Perfect Tense

This is not a difficult tense. It simply indicates that at a point of future time an event will be in the past:

By ten o'clock he *will have been* here two hours.

You *will have finished* that novel tomorrow.

There are many occasions when it is possible to use either the Future or the Future Perfect. For example, in the second example above the Future is possible:

You *will finish* that novel tomorrow.

The difference is simply that when we use the Future Perfect we are viewing the event from the future, whereas when we use the Future we are viewing the event from now. If we use a verb like *be*, as in the first example above, we are clearly viewing the event from the future and looking back on something which has been going on in the past, and therefore the only tense we can use is the Future Perfect.

Look at some more examples:

We *shall have revised* all the tenses by the end of the term.

They *will have played* all the other teams when they meet us next Saturday.

She *will have made* three dresses this month when she finishes the one she is making now.

There is also a *Future Perfect Continuous* tense, but it is rarely used. It simply indicates that an activity or state viewed in the future as past will have been going on continuously:

We *shall have been living* in this town five months next June.

He *will have been studying* French six years next summer.

EXERCISE 25

Change the infinitives in the following sentences to the Future Perfect. In which cases would the Future tense be possible?

1 By six o'clock tomorrow I (travel) over a thousand kilometres by land and sea.
2 The rain (stop) by the time we reach the town.
3 My brother (take) his degree before I leave school.
4 When he has finished the novel he is writing, he already (write) ten books.
5 I (do) this exercise on the Future Perfect in a few minutes' time.
6 It is expected that man (land) on several planets by the end of this century.
7 By the time he has repaid the loan the value of money (fall).
8 His sister (cook) the meal before he gets home.
9 When my uncle, who is a pilot, flies to England next Thursday, he (fly) over 500,000 kilometres since he qualified.
10 We (play) thirty matches when the football season ends next Saturday.

9 The Conditional Tense and Conditional Sentences

The distinction between *should* and *would* in the Conditional tense is disappearing. Most people now use *would* for all persons, although purists insist on *should* with I and we. (See p. 17 for a similar note on *shall* and *will*.)

The chief use of the Conditional tense is in a main clause when a condition is made in a dependent clause or an infinitive phrase:

We *would be able* to start the game if my brother came.

    (Main clause)   (Conditional clause)

To leave school now *would be* a mistake.

    (Infinitive phrase)   (Conditional clause)

Sometimes the condition is understood and not expressed. A very common instance of this – and one that leads to many mistakes – is in expressions like:

I *would like* to introduce our speaker.

Here the words *if I have your permission,* or *if you will allow me to* are understood although they would not normally be expressed. *I would like, I should like* and *I'd like* are polite ways of saying *I wish* and can never be shortened to *I like.*

Three Kinds of Condition

The difficulty with this tense is that there are three main kinds of condition requiring different tense sequences. Consider these three sentences:

If Tom goes to London, he will study law.

If Tom went to London, he would study law.

If Tom had gone to London, he would have studied law.

The *first* sentence implies that it is quite possible that Tom will go to London. This is known as an **open** or **likely** condition.

The *second* sentence implies that Tom is unlikely to go to London. This is known as an **unlikely** condition.

The *third* sentence is purely hypothetical. The sentence implies that Tom did not go to London and did not study law. This is known as an **unfulfilled** or **rejected** condition.

The above three sentences contain the tenses that are typical of the three kinds of condition. In table form these tenses are:

Kind of Condition	Tense in Conditional Clause	Tense in Main Clause
open	present	future
unlikely	past simple	conditional
rejected	past perfect	perfect conditional

Since the tense shows the sense there are many possible variations on these tense sequences. It is advisable, however, to be very careful about using sequences other than those shown above.

Avoid the common mistake of thinking that the Conditional tense is used in the conditional clause. The Conditional and Perfect Conditional are found only in main clauses for Unlikely and Rejected conditions respectively. If you come across a sentence like:

If he *would come* with me, I should be very glad.

The *would* of the conditional clause is being used in a special way to mean *was willing*.

Note that conditional sentences containing a Past Perfect can begin with *had* followed by the subject; in this case no *if* is used:

Had he seen the hole, he would not have fallen into it.

Other words introducing conditional clauses and requiring the above tense sequences are: *even if, suppose that, supposing that, assuming that, on condition that, provided that, as long as. Unless* means almost the same as *if not* but is rather more emphatic. *Unless* is extremely rare in Rejected conditions.

A singular subject of a conditional clause can take *were*:

If he *were* ill, who would take his place?

Was would not be incorrect. A very common use of *were* with a singular subject is in the expression *if I were you*. (Used in this way *were* is not the plural but a relic of a verb form called the subjunctive, now happily almost vanished from the language.)

EXERCISE 26

Change the infinitives in brackets to the most suitable tenses:

1 If the weather had been finer, the match (take place).

2 If the rains come early next year, there (be) a good harvest.
3 If he gets married this year, he (need) a higher salary.
4 He (visit) the dentist if he had toothache.
5 If the servant hadn't swept the floor, the master (be angry).
6 The crop would have been harvested before now if there (be) good weather.
7 If his brother had been driving, the accident (not happen).
8 If he is fit, he (play) for the school team on Saturday.
9 The electricity supply would fail if the workers at the power station (go on strike).
10 The architect would have designed a more expensive house if the owners (agree) to pay.
11 The captain will travel in the referee's car if there (be) no room on the bus.
12 The headmaster would announce a holiday if he (have) the permission of the Ministry.
13 There (be) a shortage of water next month unless it rains.
14 If he read the newspaper, he (know) an agreement has been signed.
15 If he (pass) the examination, he will be promoted.
16 If the gardener does not water the flowers, they (die).
17 His father would have visited the school if he (know) his son was in trouble.
18 If he referred to the dictionary more often, he (not make) so many spelling mistakes.
19 The editor of the school magazine will accept your article if you (shorten) it.
20 If he didn't work so hard, he (not be) so successful.
21 Our history teacher will not give us a test unless he (suspect) we have not read the last chapter.
22 He would leave school this term if he (find) a good job.
23 The student (be expelled) if he had stolen the encyclopaedias.
24 A war (break out) if the United Nations had not intervened.
25 If he knew his father was ill, he (go) home at once.
26 If he knows there will be a test next week, he (spend) the weekend revising.
27 If the main speaker (make) a convincing speech, the motion would have been carried by a large majority.
28 If our team won the match next Saturday, we (be) the league champions.
29 The Secretary-General of the United Nations (fly) to the scene of the conflict if he thought his presence would help.
30 Had there been a bed available, my brother (go) into hospital last week.

EXERCISE 27

Complete the following sentences:
  1 If I told my father, ...
  2 If he saves enough money, ...

3 I will give him the book if . . .
4 The harvest would have been better if . . .
5 If he spent a year in France, . . .
6 If he marries my sister, . . .
7 You would have a good view of the town if . . .
8 If I meet him, . . .
9 If I had caught the bus, . . .
10 I would be able to read his letter if . . .
11 If he bought a car, . . .
12 If it hadn't rained all last night, . . .
13 I will buy a copy of that magazine if . . .
14 We would be able to see the way if . . .
15 I will have time to finish this exercise if . . .
16 The headmaster would have expelled that student if . . .
17 If you go there, . . .
18 There would have been a serious accident if . . .
19 If I had a bicycle, . . .
20 The school would have closed down if . . .

EXERCISE 28
Which statements are true? (One or more in each case.)
1. If they had gone to the village, they would not have met my uncle.
This sentence tells us:
   A They did not go to the village.
   B They went to the village in order to meet my uncle.
   C They went to the village but they did not meet my uncle. .
   D They went to the village and they met my uncle.
   E They should have gone to the village but they did not.
2. If he had been warned about the crocodiles, he would not have gone swimming.
This sentence tells us:
   A He was warned about the crocodiles.
   B He went swimming.
   C He did not want to go swimming.
   D He was attacked by crocodiles.
   E He did not go swimming because he had been warned about the crocodiles.
3. If Mary gets married this year, she will be the first member of her family to marry before the age of sixteen.
This sentence tells us:
   A Mary is already married.
   B Mary will get married this year.
   C Mary is not more than sixteen.

D Mary is the youngest member of her family.

E All the other members of Mary's family are married.

4. If any of the candidates cheated, they would be disqualified.

This sentence tells us:

A Some of the candidates cheated.

B Some of the candidates tried to cheat.

C None of the candidates cheated.

D Any candidates who cheated would be disqualified.

E Many candidates were disqualified for cheating.

5. Francis would have saved more money if he had known he would not get the scholarship.

This sentence tells us:

A Francis saved no money.

B Francis got the scholarship.

C Francis did not know he would not get the scholarship.

D Francis had enough money even though he did not get the scholarship.

E Francis wanted to save more money but was unable to.

6. John would not have read the book even if it had been available.

This sentence tells us:

A John did not read the book.

B The book was available.

C The book was not available because John was reading it.

D The reason why John did not read the book was that it was not available.

E John wanted to read the book but it was not available.

7. He would still be living in Ghana if his father had not died.

This sentence tells us:

A He still lives in Ghana.

B Both he and his father used to live in Ghana.

C His father is dead.

D He wishes he were still living in Ghana.

E He would leave Ghana if his father died.

8. If Ibrahim writes to his father about his school fees, he will receive the money next week.

This sentence tells us:

A Ibrahim has written to his father about his school fees.

B Ibrahim must pay his school fees next week.

C Ibrahim will write to his father about his school fees.

D Ibrahim could receive the money next week.

9. If Ibrahim wrote a letter to his father about his school fees, he would receive the money next week.

This sentence tells us:

A Ibrahim wrote to his father about his school fees.

B Ibrahim is going to write to his father about his school fees.

C Ibrahim will not receive the money next week.

D Ibrahim might not write a letter to his father about his school fees.

10. If Ibrahim had written to his father about his school fees, he would have received the money by now.

This sentence tells us:

A Ibrahim did not write to his father about his school fees.

B Ibrahim wrote to his father about his school fees but without success.

C Ibrahim may yet receive the money from his father.

D Ibrahim's father refused to send him the money.

10 Some Other Uses of 'should' and 'would'

Should can be used with all persons to express obligation:

We *should* think over what he has said.

You *should* let him know at once.

They *should* help their parents.

Should is used in clauses of purpose:

He spent several hours on the essay so that he *should* have a good chance of winning the competition.

Would is common in polite requests:

Would you like to come to our party?

Would you let me have your reply as soon as possible?

Would not can mean refused to:

They *would not* help us.

She *would not* agree.

Would is the past of will when it means insist on:

He was told several times that unripe bananas were bad for him, but he *would* eat them (See note on *will*, p. 19)

Would can be used to express past habits:

When he was young he *would* get up at five every morning.

(It is similar to *used to* (see page 13) but it can only be used for repeated actions and not for states:

She *used to* own her own house)

EXERCISE 29

Write five sentences using *should* to express obligation.

EXERCISE 30

Write five sentences using *should* in clauses of purpose.

EXERCISE 31

Write five sentences using *would* in polite requests.

EXERCISE 32

Write five sentences using *would not* with the meaning *refused to*.

EXERCISE 33

Write five sentences using *would* with the meaning *insisted on*.

EXERCISE 34

Write five sentences using *would* to show past habit.

EXERCISE 35

Supply *should* or *would* as required in the following sentences.

1 ... you please let us have your decision soon?
2 We set out early so that we ... arrive in good time.
3 They ... not listen to our advice, and they had to suffer the consequences.
4 They ... listen to our advice since we know what we are talking about.
5 Although we tried hard to persuade him, he ... not come with us.
6 ... you be so kind as to lend me your pen?
7 Secondary students of English ... spend several hours a week reading.
8 He ... go out without his raincoat even though we told him it was going to rain.
9 In former times tribal chiefs ... settle disputes of all kinds.
10 We ... pay our school fees by next Monday.

EXERCISE 36 (Revision of all Tenses)

Change the infinitives in brackets to the most suitable tenses:

1 He (give) us another opportunity if we had tried harder.
2 She (be) married ten years next August.
3 People (become) tired more quickly at high altitudes.
4 My brother (be) in the Army five years in 1987.
5 He just (take) one degree and is planning to take another.
6 Our cook (prepare) the meal all day long and it isn't ready yet.
7 If he (fall) from that window, he would be killed.
8 While she (drive) to her office, she saw an accident.
9 We now (do) number 9 of this exercise.
10 If he (come) after eight, he will find we have left without him.
11 When she (arrive), tell her there was a telephone message for her.
12 Nigeria (be) independent since 1960.
13 Nowadays most countries (be) members of the United Nations.
14 He (not hear) of Einstein before I gave him a book on relativity.
15 He (study) in England for several years when he had to return home.
16 Easter (not come) on the same date every year.
17 Whenever we went to that restaurant the food (be) bad.
18 Exactly a year ago I (work) for the entrance examination.
19 When I went into the room I saw that many improvements (be) made since I was there last.

20 He can't buy a new jacket because he (not have) any money now.
21 As I (read) that book I can tell you all you want to know.
22 The Second World War (last) for six years.
23 He (go) to the party if he had been invited.
24 This exercise (appear) to be easier than it is.
25 "What were you doing in that room?" "I (look) for my pen."
26 I'd like to go out but I (not finish) this exercise yet.
27 What you (do) if I can't lend you the money?
28 They (tear) down the fence last week because it was so ugly.
29 She (marry) him if he asked her to.
30 "Where is your brother?" "He (work) in the field."

EXERCISE 37 (Revision of all Tenses)
Change the infinitives in brackets to the most suitable tenses:
  1 Although he just (clean) the windows for over an hour, they are still dirty.
  2 He (be) in this country over twenty years next July.
  3 I used to think he was clever, but now I (think) he is stupid.
  4 Now that you have explained your reasons so clearly I (understand) them.
  5 Although he just (look up) the word in the dictionary, he has misspelt it.
  6 We (use) the Present Perfect tense for past events closely connected with the present.
  7 The north wind (blow) since last month, but we hope it will stop soon.
  8 The coffee (boil). I can hear it.
  9 I (spend) the money on clothes unless you tell me not to.
10 It (rain) for a whole week tomorrow.
11 He (study) at London University when he was a young man.
12 He would have been able to complete his studies if he (save) more money.
13 I can't bear that man. He always (complain) about something.
14 The clouds (gather) since this morning. It will rain soon.
15 I would tell you his name if I (know) it.
16 The Prime Minister (fly) to Cairo next month.
17 He doesn't know what 'incompetence' (mean).
18 "Get some iodine quickly. A wasp just (sting) me."
19 Our team (withdraw) from the competition over a month ago.
20 (Help) me do this exercise? I am finding it very difficult.
21 Iron (expand) when it is heated.
22 These two girls (resemble) each other much more when they were younger.
23 He didn't like English food at first, but now he (like) it very much.
24 She (look) the word up in the dictionary if I hadn't hidden it.
25 I (intend) to go to London for the last month, but I haven't been able to.
26 When I told her what a good film was on at the cinema, she (want) to go.
27 She used to be poor, but now she (own) two houses.
28 In a few minutes he (sleep) fifteen hours. I think we should wake him up now.

29 I (come) on foot if it isn't raining.

30 He (tear) open the letter as soon as I gave it to him.

11 The Passive

The passive is formed by using the verb *to be* followed by the past participle:

The house *was destroyed* by fire.

Portuguese *is spoken* in Brazil.

The regulation *has been changed*.

The building *will be completed* next month.

The radio must *be repaired*.

He enjoyed *being flattered*.

(In the last example but one we have the infinitive form of the passive – *be* + past participle; in the last example the -ing form of the passive – the -ing form of *be* + past participle.)

Not every sentence in the active can be changed to the passive. The passive should be restricted to these three uses:

1. When the performer of the action is unknown:

   His father was killed in the war.

   My pen has been stolen.

2. When it is unnecessary to state who the performer of the action is:

   Arabic is spoken in Morocco.

   This book was printed in England.

3. When we wish to draw attention to the subject rather than the agent:

   President Kennedy was killed by a bullet.

   His sister was knocked down by a bus.

(In the first and second pairs of examples no mention is made of the performer of the action. It would therefore be quite unrealistic to try to render the same ideas in the active.)

EXERCISE 38 (Revision of all Tenses and the Passive)

Write out the following sentences using the active or passive as required and the correct tenses:

1 You (surprise) to hear that I got the job, weren't you? I (interview) only ten days ago and I didn't think I (make) a good impression. I must (give) good references by the headmaster and Mr. Williams. I (take up) the post on the first of next month. The salary of the post (raise) only a month ago and I (pay) much more than I need. My brother will ask me for a loan when he (hear) I (give) the job.

2 The results of the examination (announce) later this month. My brother (expect) he has passed, but he (warn) by his teachers last week to expect the worst. Nobody (exempt) from the final last·year as the general standard (consider) to be too low.

3 When the cinema (collapse) last night several people (kill). Many more (kill) if the tragedy (occur) half an hour later when the main film was due to (show). The owner of the cinema (tell) months ago that the structure (be) faulty and that he (risk) the lives of hundreds of people if he (not spend) money on repairs.

4 The game (begin) at two o'clock and by half past two five goals (score) – four by our team. When the referee (blow) the whistle for half-time, we (lead) by six goals to one. Later our goal-keeper (injure) and we (do) badly during the rest of the game. In the end the game (draw) six-six.

5 Latin (speak) by the Romans, who (take) the language with them to several other countries which they (conquer). In these countries Latin (undergo) various changes and eventually (develop) into French, Spanish, Portuguese and Roumanian. In Italy, too, Latin (evolve) and although Italian (resemble) Latin more than any other modern language (do), it cannot (understand) by an Italian who (not study) the language.

6 English and French now (speak) in many parts of Africa. A knowledge of these languages (enable) people to communicate with each other all over the continent. In some countries laws (pass) making one of these languages the official first or second language, and there are few countries where one of them (not use) for commerce.

7 John (suffer) from a bad cold for several days now. He (oblige) to stay indoors over the weekend and (look after) by his wife, but he (go) to work yesterday although he (advise) by the doctor to stay at home for a few more days. His work cannot (do) by anybody else and he (be) very conscientious.

8 During the last war books (make) of cheap paper. A law (pass) forcing publishers to economise. This law (not repeal) until after the war. Books can still (find) that (publish) at that time. The binding (be) inferior and very often the paper (become) discoloured.

9 Before a house (build) secure foundations have (lay). Many unwise builders (ruin) by not spending enough money on the foundations. Simply because the foundations cannot (see) by prospective buyers (not mean) that they (not be) the most important part of the building.

10 In recent years there (be) great advances in technology. Jobs which (do) by hand ten years ago can now (do) by machines. Unfortunately in some countries this development (cause) unemployment but most people (believe) now that it (benefit) economies in the long term.

11 My father (spend) many hours working in the garden recently. It (neglect) while we (be) on holiday for two months. Weeds (grow up) everywhere and because it (rain) heavily the grass (be) very tall when we (return). Some of the plants (destroy) by dogs and we (have to) spend a lot of money on new ones in the last two weeks.

12 Roads and railways must (build) in developing countries so that earth-moving equipment for the establishment of industries can easily

(transport). When the industries (establish), the products can (distribute) and (export) only if the roads and railways well (maintain).

13 The judge (tell) that the accused man (imprison) three times before. He said that this time he (discharge) him since he (not convince) that he (be) guilty. He (sentence) to several years' imprisonment if he (convict) on that occasion.

14 When a person (inoculate) disease germs (introduce) into the body so that he (have) a mild attack of the disease to prevent him being liable to a severe one. Inoculation for smallpox first (practise) in Turkey and (use) in England in 1717.

15 If you (wish) to learn a language quickly, begin with the spoken language. When you (be able) to express yourself simply, you (should) write down what you already (teach) to speak. It (prove) that people who (approach) a language in this way (make) much more rapid progress than those who (teach) to write from the very first lesson.

16 Mr. Okala (appoint) the manager of that company last year because he (make) a reputation as a good administrator in his previous posts. His work in his present post (be) very difficult since the day he (take) over as the company already (lose) a lot of business to competitors.

17 When Usman (be) a student in England, he (spend) a lot of his time working in libraries. The room which he (share) with another student (heat) only by a small electric fire and he (have) not enough money to pay for the electricity. He frequently (ask) his parents to send him more money, but they not (able) to.

18 Irrigation now (use) in several parts of the world. Countries which already (develop) extensive systems of irrigation are Egypt, the Sudan, India, the United States of America and Australia. In the Sudan the Gezira cotton scheme, on which the economy of the country virtually (depend), (make) possible several years ago by irrigation. Irrigation not (be) new: it (practise) thousands of years ago in the Nile region.

19 Although it (prove) that there (be) a definite link between cigarette smoking and lung cancer, more cigarettes (smoke) now than ever before. In the United States the words 'Health Hazard' must (print) on each packet of cigarettes so that people (know) that they (endanger) their health when they (smoke). Many cigarette manufacturers (look) still for some means of removing the danger, but it (be) unlikely they (be) successful in the near future.

20 Magnets (know) since classical times; their name (derive) from Magnes in Greece, where magnet stones (find) at one time. The earth (behave) like a huge magnet, and this fact (make) possible the magnetic compass. The nineteenth-century British scientist, Michael Faraday, (make) use of the principle of magnetism in the dynamo.

21 A professor of mathematics (invite) to attend a conference in another

country and his flight (book) for him. He (go) to the airline office some days before he (be) due to fly and (say) that he (wish) to cancel the flight because he (calculate) that the chances that the plane (destroy) by a bomb explosion (be) one in ten thousand, and that (not be) a risk he (prepare) to take. The clerk (be) a little surprised at his reasoning but (not attempt) to argue with him.

A day before the conference (start) the professor (return) to the airline office. He (ask) if he (can) have the original booking after all. The clerk (remind) him that he (say) he (be) afraid there (be) a bomb on the plane. The professor (reply) that he (make) further calculations and (assure) himself that the chances of there being two bombs on the plane (be) the square of ten thousand, and that (be) a small risk. The clerk (ask) him how he (can) be sure there (be) one bomb on the plane. The professor (annoy) at what (appear) to him to be a stupid question, and (say), "I (take) the precaution of carrying one bomb in my case when I (fly) tomorrow." The clerk, finding it difficult to suppress a smile, (book) the professor on the plane and (wish) him a good trip.

TEST ON ALL TENSES AND THE PASSIVE

Write out each sentence using the most suitable tense from those supplied:
1 I know that he ... in the library at this moment.
   A has worked   B is working   C works   D was working   E has been working
2 His father ... as a gardener when he was young, but now he is a driver.
   A had worked   B has worked   C used to work   D would work
   E had been working
3 John ... the examination if he had worked harder.
   A would pass   B will pass   C was passing   D would have passed
   E had passed
4 Two thousand years ago Latin ... in Italy.
   A was spoken   B had been spoken   C has been spoken   D is being spoken   E would be spoken
5 He ... on his history essay all yesterday morning.
   A used to work   B had worked   C has worked   D was working
   E has been working
6 The fishermen ... nothing when they returned home.
   A were catching   B caught   C had caught   D would catch   E have caught
7 He ... . by the police once already.
   A is being warned   B has been warned   C is warned   D has warned
   E warned
8 At this moment I ... that we have a good chance of victory.

A was feeling   B am feeling   C had been feeling   D feel   E felt

9 He will have visited all the capitals of Europe when he ... to Oslo.

   A had gone   B went   C goes   D will have gone   E will go

10 She ... hard since the beginning of this term.

   A had been working   B has been working   C worked   D is working
   E was working

11 When he was a young man he ... to be a doctor.

   A wants   B would want   C wanted   D has wanted

12 At the end of the day I ... eight hours' work.

   A shall be doing   B shall have done   C shall do   D shall have been
   doing.

13 Before I woke up the burglars ... most of my possessions.

   A have taken   B were taking   C had taken   D will take   E are taking

14 All candidates ... to take eight subjects.

   A required   B are required   C have required   D being required
   E requiring

15 I would have told you if I ...

   A was knowing   B have known   C were knowing   D had known
   E had been knowing

16 We have done a lot of work on the tenses lately and we now ... most of
   the rules.

   A were understanding   B understand   C understood   D will understand
   E are understanding

17 If I ... rich enough, I would get married.

   A had been   B were   C have been   D am   E will be

18 He ... a novel when I entered the room.

   A is reading   B has read   C was reading   D has been reading
   E will read

19 The pupils ... home before the storm began.

   A have been sent   B were sent   C were being sent   D were sending
   E have been sending

20 I ... Chemistry ever since I came to this school.

   A had been studying   B was studying   C am studying   D studied
   E have been studying

21 A new translation of the Bible ... by some British scholars.

   A is making   B had been made   C making   D made   E is being
   made

22 We ... in this house five years next April.

   A shall be living   B shall have lived   C have lived   D shall live
   E live

23 He ... an hour's French every day now that the examination is
   approaching.

   A used to do   B uses to do   C is doing   D did   E was doing

24 Since last year the Principal ... a history of the college.

A has been writing   B is writing   C will write   D writes   E wrote

25 My brother now ... to go to Nsukka to study law.

A wishes   B is wishing   C has wished   D has been wishing   E was wishing

26 Our rent ... by the landlord every month.

A collected   B had collected   C is collected   D being collected   E collects

27 We shall welcome him if he ...

A came   B comes   C had come   D was coming   E has been coming

28 He ... the meeting if we had written to him.

A will have attended   B will attend   C had attended   D would attend   E would have attended

29 No sooner ... the door than the thief fled.

A had I opened   B was I opening   C opened I   D would I be opening   E have I been opening

30 Our teacher ... us a test when the Principal entered.

A has given   B gives   C was giving   D will give

31 He ... captain of the football team this year if he had not been ill last November.

A will be   B will have been   C would have been   D shall be

32 The players ... to report at three o'clock.

A told   B have told   C tell   D were told   E are telling

33 They ... there four years when the roof fell in.

A lived   B were living   C have been living   D had been living   E will have lived

34 The teacher who came to this school last month ... a history of Nigeria for the last two years.

A wrote   B is writing   C writes   D had been writing   E has been writing

35 I shall have read all the works of Dickens when I ... 'The Mystery of Edwin Drood'.

A shall finish   B shall have finished   C finished   D am finishing   E finish

36 He ... early when he lived in the country.

A has got up   B used to get up   C had got up   D was getting up   E had been getting up

37 Your suggestion ... by the committee at this moment.

A discussing   B is being discussed   C discussed   D discusses   E is discussed

38 I ... my composition just as the invigilator said 'Pens down'.

A used to finish   B finished   C have finished   D had been finishing.

39 Nowadays his father ... to work by car.

A goes   B used to go   C has gone   D went   E was going
40 They ... to the cinema if they had known it was the last night of the film.
   A will go   B would have gone   C would go   D went   E had gone
41 Mr. Okongwu ... headmaster of this school ten years next December.
   A was   B will have been   C has been   D will be   E is
42 All the envelopes ... by the new clerk.
   A had addressed   B addressed   C addressing   D were addressing
   E were addressed
43 When he ... to the university, he will visit us less often.
   A goes   B will have gone   C went   D would go
44 We ... television for two hours when you knocked at our door.
   A watched   B had been watching   C were watching   D have watched
45 He ... an hour's algebra every morning before coming to school, but now
   he has to leave home so early that this is impossible.
   A has done   B was doing   C used to do   D had done
46 The Principal promised that he ... the Ministry next week.
   A will visit   B would visit   C has visited   D will have visited
   E visits
47 That desk ... several times this year.
   A has been repaired   B has repaired   C repaired   D is being repaired
   E had been repaired
48 Whenever he ... home, he takes his parents a present.
   A went   B has been   C has gone   D will go   E goes
49 I ... for four posts without success and now I am planning to continue my
   studies.
   A apply   B am applying   C have applied   D was applying   E had
   applied
50 We ... there for six years when the earthquake occurred.
   A were living   B would live   C had been living   D have lived
51 We ... on this exercise for several minutes now.
   A were working   B have been working   C worked   D are working
52 Most of the city ... by an earthquake in 1906.
   A destroyed   B was destroyed   C had been destroyed   D was being
   destroyed   E has destroyed
53 When John was in the first year he ... hard.
   A has worked   B would have worked   C used to work   D has been
   working
54 He ... by airmail if he knew we wanted the information urgently.
   A will reply   B would reply   C would have replied   D has replied
55 Next summer he ... his secondary education.
   A will have completed   B completed   C would complete   D shall
   have completed   E was completing
56 My young brother ... so much noise while I was trying to listen to the

music that I could not enjoy it.

A had made B will be making C had been making D was making
E has made

57 He ... a teacher for twenty years when he became headmaster of our school.

A is B was C was being D had been E has been

58 Our baby ... by our mother tonight.

A looked after B looking after C looks after D is being looked after
E has been looked after

59 We shall write to him when he ... to his village.

A had returned   B is returned   C shall return   D will return
E returns

60 The telephone ... in the nineteenth century and is now used in every country of the world.

A has been invented B had been invented C was invented D was being invented E would have been invented

B Other Verb Difficulties

1 Verbs Followed by '-ing' Words

There is a common sentence pattern:

He enjoyed reading that novel. (Verb + -ing word)

The following is a list of verbs which take -ing words:

admit	He admitted stealing the book. (Note: the passive takes the infinitive: He was admitted *to be* a criminal.)
appreciate	She appreciated having the oppportunity to visit her brother.
avoid	I avoided crossing the road because of the traffic.
consider	He considered leaving school when he was sixteen. (Note: the passive takes the infinitive: She was considered *to be* the most beautiful girl in the village.)
delay	I delayed replying to his letter.
deny	He denied having been outside the compound.
detest	I detest writing compositions about subjects I am not interested in.
dislike	I dislike having to spend my weekends in school.
enjoy	We enjoyed seeing that film.
escape	My brother escaped being hurt when the car crashed.

excuse	He was excused arriving late. (In the active form the construction is usually: verb + possessive (or object) + *-ing*: I excused his (him) arriving late.)
finish	He finished reading that book before I did.
forgive	He was forgiven not coming since he wasn't well. (In the active form the construction is the same as *excuse* above.)
give up	She gave up writing poetry.
go on	He went on writing after he was told to stop. (Note the expression: He went on to say ...)
imagine	Imagine seeing a ghost in your bedroom! (Note: the passive takes the infinitive.)
keep on	He kept on asking silly questions.
leave off	It left off raining at five o'clock.
mention	The headmaster mentioned receiving some new books.
mind	Do you mind switching on the radio?
postpone	The official postponed visiting the school.
practise	He practised typing all yesterday afternoon.
put off	They put off coming to see us because of the weather.
recollect	Do you recollect seeing him?
resent	She resented being told to keep quiet.
resist	He resisted eating another cake.
suggest	My friend suggested playing tennis tomorrow.
stop	He stopped smoking on the advice of his doctor.
understand	My father does not understand my wanting to go to the university.
be worth	It's worth asking him his opinion.

Make up your own sentences using each of the above verbs with an *-ing* word.

2 Verbs Followed by the Infinitive

Certain verbs are followed by an infinitive, giving the pattern:

She hoped to find a job as a nurse.

Verbs of this kind are:

care	He didn't care to come to our party.
decide	He decided to leave the meeting early.
deserve	He deserved to win the race. (Note: *-ing* can be used with passive meaning; he deserves punishing.)
expect	I expected to receive some money today.
forget	He forgot to bring his pen.
hope	He hoped to live by writing plays.
learn	He learnt to ride a bicycle when he was six. (Note: *learn* may be

	followed by a skill – typing, singing, etc.)
mean	(when it is the equivalent of 'intend') He meant to go away for a holiday last week.
promise	She promised to meet me yesterday.
want	He wanted to go to America. (Note: like *deserve*, the *-ing* form can be used with passive meaning, e.g. *The grass wants cutting*.)
wish	They wished to stay in our house.

Make up your own sentences, using each of the above verbs with an infinitive.

3 Verbs Followed by an Object + Infinitive

Some verbs require an object before the infinitive:

His father persuaded him to apologise.

(In the passive, of course, the object is not found:

He was persuaded to apologise by his father.)

Such verbs are:

advise	His uncle advised him to take the examination again.
allow	The teacher allowed us to use a dictionary.
cause	The rain caused us to cancel the match.
command	The officer commanded his troops to advance.
encourage	His success encouraged him to continue his studies.
force	The policeman forced the thief to tell the truth.
get	We got him to agree with us in the end.
instruct	The manager instructed the clerk to write a letter.
invite	We invited a well-known writer to address our Society.
oblige	Bad weather obliged us to postpone the visit.
order	The doctor ordered him to rest.
persuade	The Chairman persuaded us to leave the matter to the next meeting.
remind	I reminded him to return his library book.
teach	My father taught me to read.
tell	I told him to spend his money wisely.
warn	The President warned the people to be prepared for food shortages.

Make up your own sentences, using each of the above verbs with an object + infinitive.

4 Verbs Followed by either Infinitive or '-ing' Word

A number of verbs can take either the infinitive or an *-ing* word without any noticeable difference in meaning. These verbs are:

attempt, begin, cease, continue, dread, hate, intend, like, love, plan, prefer, propose, start.

If *allow* or *permit* is followed by an object, or is in the passive, it takes the infinitive. If it does not have another object, it may be followed by the *-ing* form.

The doctor allowed him to eat.

But he was allowed to eat meat.

but The new assistant does not allow talking in the library.

The headmaster permitted us to go home early.

We were permitted to go home early.

but The rules do not permit smoking in the cinema.

Remember, forget, try, regret and *mean* have somewhat different meanings according to whether they are followed by the infinitives or the gerund:

I remembered to go to his village.

(= I did not forget to go his village.)

I remember going to his village.

(= I recall going to his village.)

I forgot to look the word up in the dictionary.

(= I didn't look the word up in the dictionary because of a lapse of memory.)

I shall never forget running that race.

(= I shall always have the memory of running that race.)

He tried to read the book.

(= He made an effort to read the book.)

He tried reading the book.

(= He sampled some of the book.)

He said he regretted to tell us the news.

(= He was sorry to tell us the news, i.e. he said this before or while actually telling us the news.)

He said he regretted telling us the news.

(= He was sorry he had told us the news.)

He meant to go to England last year.

(= He intended to go to England last year.)

This means doing the work again.

(= This makes it necessary to do the work again.)

5 Verbs Followed by Object + Present Participle or Infinitive

Some verbs can be followed by an object + a present participle or an infinitive. The use of the present participle implies that the action described by it continued after the action of the main verb, the infinitive that it was completed during the action of the main verb.

feel	I felt the water getting cold.
	(i.e. it probably continued to get cold after I got out of it.)
	I felt the water get cold.
	(i.e. it reached its minimum temperature while I was still in it.)
hear	She heard him playing the tune.
	(i.e. she did not hear him play all of the tune.)
	She heard him play the tune.
	(i.e. she heard him play all the tune.)
listen to	We listened to the headmaster reading out the results.
	We listened to the headmaster read out the results.
notice	I noticed the weather changing.
	I noticed the weather change.
observe	The students observed the chemical dissolving.
	The students observed the chemical dissolve.
see	I saw the train arriving.
	I saw the train arrive.
watch	He watched me playing tennis.
	He watched me play tennis.

Note: The possessive is never used before the present participle or the infinitive in this construction.

Make up your own sentences, using each of the above verbs with an object + present participle and with an object + infinitive.

6 '-ing' Words with Prepositions

After prepositions the *-ing* is used:

Poverty prevented him *from* continuing his education.

After attending the lecture, we went home.

Instead *of* going to school, he studied at home.

7 '-ing' Words with Possessive or Object

Pronouns and proper names can come before an *-ing*:

I don't like *his* interfering in our affairs.

I don't like *John's* interfering in our affairs.

He appreciated *her* correcting his work.

He appreciated *Mary's* correcting his work.

Alternatively, an object can be used:

I don't like *him* interfering in our affairs.

I don't like *John* interfering in our affairs.

He appreciated *her* correcting his work.
He appreciated *Mary* correcting his work.

EXERCISE 39 (Revision of *-ing*, Present Participle and Infinitive)
Change the verb in brackets to *-ing*, present participle or infinitive as required:
  1 We hope (pass) the final exam.
  2 They avoided (pay) the fine.
  3 She consider (leave) school when she was sixteen.
  4 We don't like his (call) on us late in the evening.
  5 We were obliged (sign) an oath before we were given the scholarship.
  6 He was encouraged (enter) the University.
  7 My cousin is looking forward to (leave) school at the end of the year.
  8 I suggested (discuss) the matter with the headmaster.
  9 The clerk was ordered (file) the letters.
 10 I enjoyed (listen) to that radio programme.
 11 I could smell the gas (escape).
 12 Do you mind (open) that window?
 13 He warned us (not buy) that house.
 14 Instead of (work) for his living he relied on charity.
 15 We all finished (write) our compositions before the bell went.
 16 The English teacher promised (give) us our final marks today.
 17 She has decided (marry) my brother.
 18 I saw the bus (arrive) and when all the passengers had got off I went home.
 19 I would appreciate (hear) from you as soon as possible.
 20 We expect her (arrive) in Nairobi at six o'clock.
 21 He practised (write) French for half an hour every day.
 22 She is accustomed (spend) her holidays at home.
 23 The chairman will object to us (leave) early.
 24 We were advised (buy) a new radio.
 25 She listened to the bird (sing).
 26 The boy denied (steal) the watch.
 27 Nobody is allowed (swim) in this lake.
 28 He delayed (give) his answer to our enquiry for several days.
 29 They have invited us (eat) with them next Wednesday.
 30 I remember (go) to a big town for the first time.
 31 Every student remembered (bring) his textbook with him and was able to
    do the exercise.
 32 The officer commanded his men (attack) the fort.
 33 He mentioned (take) the examination but did not say if he had passed it.
 34 He deserves (get) a good job.
 35 I can understand him (be afraid) of his uncle.
 36 Without (take) care very little of lasting value can be achieved.
 37 They missed (see) the film.

38 I was taught (ride) a horse last summer.

39 The weather caused us (change) our plans.

40 I listened to him (play) the piano but went away before he had finished.

41 He has given up (study) English.

42 I suggested (leave) the matter until tomorrow.

43 He objected to my (address) him by his first name.

44 The enemy forced our troops (surrender).

45 As cigarettes affected his breathing, the doctor told him to try (smoke) a pipe.

46 She tried (do) the exercise but found it too difficult.

47 It is worth (wait) until he comes.

48 His parents would not agree to his (leave) school.

49 He was persuaded (lend) me some money.

50 Nobody was permitted (write) the answers in pencil.

51 The rules do not permit (smoke).

52 She kept on (annoy) me.

53 Hark at the dog (bark).

54 I meant (give) you the book yesterday but I forgot to.

55 I felt the rain (fall) so I quickly put on my coat.

56 The boy admitted (break) the window.

57 Everybody dislikes (pay) taxes.

58 Forgive me (ask) you, but have you forgotten my invitation?

59 His father reminded him (post) the letter.

60 We got the policeman (let) us in after he had seen our passes.

8 Participial Phrases

Checking over his work, the student found several mistakes.

The words in italics are known as a present participial phrase.

In using a participial phrase one must be sure the performer of the action of the verb in participial form is the subject of the attached clause. Do not write sentences like:

Driving along the road, a goat was knocked down.

Clearly, it is not the goat that was driving. We should write:

Driving along the road, we knocked a goat down.

(Or, not using a participial phrase:

As we were driving along the road, we knocked a goat down.)

EXERCISE 40

Join the following sentences, making the one *in italics* a present participial phrase:

1 *He wished to earn money to support his parents.* He left school at sixteen.

2 *The student hoped to catch up with his work.* The student who had been absent for six weeks got up every morning at five o'clock.

3 *I looked up the meaning of a word in the dictionary.* I found several pages were missing.

4 *He was sitting at the back of the hall.* He heard very little of the lecture.

5 *She found that biology did not interest her.* She decided to drop the subject.

6 *The teacher knew that there would be a free afternoon.* He gave us extra homework.

7 *She played tennis every afternoon.* She soon lost weight.

8 *I looked out of the window.* I noticed that it was raining.

9 *He was digging in his garden.* He found a box of coins.

10 *The servant swept under the carpet.* He found a ring.

If we want to show that one action took place before the other we can use another participial construction: 'HAVING' + PAST PARTICIPLE:

He had been a teacher for thirty-five years. He retired.

Having been a teacher for thirty-five years, he retired.

Beware of repeating the subject unnecessarily in such sentences:

The headmaster, having warned the boy on three occasions, decided to expel him.

It would be quite wrong to put *he* before *decided*.

EXERCISE 41

Join the following sentences, making the one *in italics* a past participial phrase:

1 *I had looked for my watch for two hours.* I gave up all hope of finding it.

2 *He had been elected to the committee of the club.* He knew he had to attend all the meetings.

3 *Mr. Yahaya had read many books on the subject.* He was able to give us an interesting talk.

4 *I had read that book before.* I didn't want to read it again.

5 *He had studied Latin.* He found Spanish an easy language to learn.

6 The student went to his desk. *He had apologised to the teacher for coming late.*

7 *She had been trained as a nurse.* She decided to study to become a doctor.

8 *The committee discussed the problem for two hours.* They could not reach agreement.

9 *He had been up all night.* He fell asleep during the morning lessons.

10 *He had studied English for five years.* He read novels with ease.

EXERCISE 42

Add to the following participial phrases so as to make sentences:

Example: Walking along the road, . . .

Walking along the road, he met his uncle.

1 Speaking in whispers, . . .

2 Searching in the dark for a torch, ...
3 Lifting up the lid of the box, ...
4 Riding his bicycle along the main road, ...
5 Running towards the goal, ...
6 Having searched for the number in the telephone directory, ...
7 Having played tennis all the afternoon, ...
8 Having finished his essay a quarter of an hour before the end of the examination, ...
9 Having saved up enough money, ...
10 Having done well at school, ...

9 'Can' and 'be able'

The difference between *can* and *be able* used in the Present tense is insignificant. (*Remember never to combine these two verbs. I can be able* is a very serious error.)

Permission

Both *can* and *could* are used to show permission.

Students *can* work in the library until ten o'clock.

I *could* go to the cinema any evening when I was a boy.

Ability

Both *could* and *was able* are used to express ability in the past; but when we want to stress the fact that an action was actually performed, we must use *was able*:

I *could* play the piano when I was quite young.

The merchant *could* make a good profit.

(In these two sentences we are interested simply in the fact that I had the ability to play the piano when I was quite young and that the merchant was in a position to make a good profit; we are not concerned with whether I actually played the piano (although I obviously did) or whether the merchant actually made a good profit.)

He *was able* to satisfy the examiners.

The horse *was able* to jump over the fence.

(In these sentences we mean that not only was something possible but that it actually took place. Not only *could* he satisfy the examiners — he actually took the examination and passed it; not only *could* the horse jump over the fence — he actually did jump over it.)

Note: There is a distinction between *can* (with future meaning) and *will be able*:

The doctor says that I *can* go back to school tomorrow.

(i.e. I have permission to go back to school tomorrow.)

I *will be able* to play football again when my leg is better.

(i.e. It will be physically possible for me to play football again when my leg is better.)

EXERCISE 43

Complete the following sentences, using *was able to*, *were able to*, *will be able to*, *shall be able to* if the idea of ability should be stressed, *could* or *can* if the sense of the sentence is permission:

1 Nobody ... leave before the end of the play because the regulations did not allow it.
2 Nobody ... leave before the end of the play because the doors were locked.
3 The dog ... come into the house as far as we are concerned.
4 The dog ... come into the house since the door was open.
5 Our captain ... (not) play last week as he was suspended by the league.
6 Our captain ... (not) play last week as he had sprained his ankle.
7 He ... to drive his car to Lagos as soon as it is repaired.
8 He ... drive his car to Lagos as soon as he gets his driving licence.
9 The chairman told the members of the committee that they ... vote during the meeting.
10 She ... do exactly as she wishes when she leaves school.
11 We ... (not) have the debate as the electricity failed.
12 Now that the hours have been changed you ... study in the library until nine o'clock.
13 His father said he ... go to the football match.
14 That boy ... run 100 metres in 10 seconds when he is older.
15 I ... buy a new jacket last week after saving up for several months.
16 Students under the age of fifteen ... enter for the examination last year.
17 That examination was so difficult that only 5 per cent of the candidates ... pass.
18 The cleaners ... not clean the classroom as it was locked.
19 The headmaster said we ... go to the cinema next Thursday.
20 When she has lived in France for a year she ... speak the language fluently.

10 'Must' and 'have to'

There is only a slight difference between *must* and *have to*: *must* implies when used with I or we that the subject is in agreement with the obligation or has even suggested it. With you *must* implies a kind of order. *Have to* is used with

I, we or you when somebody other than the speaker is responsible for the compulsion. (With he, she, it and they the distinction between *must* and *has to/have to* is insignificant.)

I *must* wear a tie when I go for the interview. (i.e. I think it would be a good idea to wear a tie when I go for the interview.

I *have to* wear a tie when I go for the interview. (i.e. I shall wear a tie when I go for the interview because it is expected of me.)

You *must* do as you are told. (i.e. You have no choice but to obey and I think you should.)

You *have to* do as you are told. (i.e. Obedience is expected of you and I have no comment to make.)

When in doubt, it is advisable to use *must* as there are few occasions when it cannot be used instead of *have to*, but there are many occasions when *have to* would be inappropriate.

Must exists only with present and future meaning. For all other tenses a form of the verb *have to* is used:

We *had to* close the windows because of the rain.

He *has had* to give up smoking.

They *would have to* move out if they didn't pay the rent.

EXERCISE 44

Which is preferable in the gaps in the following sentences – *must* or *have to*? The sense of the sentence is given in brackets.

1 I ... get up very early tomorrow morning. (I know that it is necessary.)
2 I ... get up very early tomorrow morning. (I resent it, but there is nothing I can do about it.)
3 You ... spend the week with us. (We want you to.)
4 You ... spend the week with us. (You have no alternative.)
5 I ... hand in my homework by tomorrow morning. (I have no choice in the matter since that is the time fixed by our teacher.)
6 I ... hand in my homework by tomorrow morning. (I know and accept that that is the latest time.)
7 He ... take this medicine three times a day. (That's what the doctor ordered and I'm only repeating what he said.)
8 He ... take this medicine three times a day. (I think it is good for him.)
9 I ... copy out this exercise again. (I feel I should since my work looks very untidy.)
10 I ... copy out this exercise again. (My teacher has told me to.)

EXERCISE 45

Change these sentences into the past, adding the adverbs of past time given in brackets:

1 I *must* revise my history notes. (last night)

2 You must visit the doctor. (last Friday)
3 John must pass an examination. (before he entered the college)
4 We must answer all the questions. (in last year's exam.)
5 I must return my library books. (last Saturday)
6 She must save some money for her holiday. (last year)
7 We must take our radio to be repaired. (on Tuesday)
8 We must get permission before leaving school. (last term)
9 I must write an article for the school magazine. (yesterday afternoon)
10 The gardener must water the garden every day. (during the dry weather)

EXERCISE 46
Expand the following into sentences containing the idea of compulsion, using the suggested tense of the verb *have to*.
Example: leave early (Past Simple)
            We had to leave early to catch the bus.
 1 complete the application form (Past Simple)
 2 read more widely (Future)
 3 write to his father (Conditional Negative)
 4 walk all the way (Present Perfect)
 5 pay his school fees (Past Simple Negative)
 6 take the examination again (Perfect Conditional)
 7 learn to write more legibly (Future)
 8 drive more carefully (Perfect Conditional)
 9 stop playing football (Present Perfect Interrogative)
10 leave school to earn his living (Future)
11 buy a new battery for his radio (Past Interrogative)
12 switch off the lights (Past Simple)
13 sweep the dormitory floor (Future)
14 mend his bicycle (Past Simple)
15 borrow money (Conditional Negative)

11 'Must not' and 'need not'

Must not is used to express an obligation not to do something; *need not* to express the absence of obligation to do something:

> Students *must not* wear jackets. (i.e. There is a rule against the wearing of jackets.)
> Students *need not* wear jackets. (i.e. Students can wear jackets if they wish to but they are not obliged to.)

Other examples:

> The patient *must not* be allowed out of the hospital.
> The patient *need not* be given another injection.

These trousers *must not* be washed in boiling water.

These trousers *need not* be shortened.

As *must not* can be used with only present and future meaning, the verb *have not to* is used for the other tenses:

She *won't have to* go into hospital.

He *didn't have to* wait long for an answer.

EXERCISE 47

Complete these sentences by supplying *must not* or *need not* as appropriate:

1 You ... make tea without first boiling the water.
2 You ... shout as I am not deaf.
3 You ... hurry as we're not late.
4 Borrowers ... keep books longer than three weeks.
5 One ... smoke at the petrol station.
6 As your hair is not very long you ... have it cut for another week.
7 You ... wear your tie to the party but you ... forget to put on a clean shirt.
8 I ... play my radio too loud or I will annoy my neighbours.
9 Women who have a profession ... get married just for the sake of money.
10 Members of the team ... train tomorrow as Saturday's match has been cancelled.
11 This boy ... take any more tablets as he is better already.
12 The dentist told me that I ... visit him again for six months but I ... eat so many sweets.
13 He ... stay too late at the dance or he will miss the last bus home.
14 You ... eat these bananas as they are not yet ripe, but you ... go hungry while we have so many oranges.
15 I ... stay talking too long or my dinner will get cold.

12 'Did not need to' and 'need not have'

He *didn't need to* come to the meeting.

He *needn't have* come to the meeting.

Both these sentences imply that it was unnecessary for him to come to the meeting. The first sentence implies that probably he did not come to the meeting because before it took place he realised his presence was not necessary. The second sentence implies that he came to the meeting and he later realised (or somebody else later realised) that it was unnecessary for him to be there.

EXERCISE 48

Supply *didn't need to* or *needn't have* and the appropriate form of the verb as required in the following sentences:

1 You ... (tell) me as I knew already.
2 She ... (ask) for a loan as some money from her father was already on the way although she didn't realise it.
3 She ... (ask) for a loan as she had plenty of money. (She knew she had plenty of money.)
4 My uncle ... (build) a new house since the one he had was big enough. (He regretted it afterwards.)
5 My uncle ... (build) a new house and decided instead simply to add two rooms to the one he already had.
6 We ... (put) more petrol in our tank since we had quite enough for the rest of the journey. (We realised it at the time.)
7 We ... (put) more petrol in our tank since we had enough for the rest of the journey. (We didn't realise it at the time.)
8 I ... (ask) permission to leave since anybody could leave whenever they liked. (I didn't know that at the time.)
9 I ... (ask) permission to leave since anybody could leave whenever they liked. (I knew I could leave.)
10 He ... (rewrite) the sentence since it was right. (It was only later when his teacher gave him back his work that he realised the original sentence was right.)

13 'Must' and 'can't' meaning 'I am sure'

A sentence like:
> He *must* earn a good salary: he lives in such an expensive house.

means: 'I am sure that he earns a good salary.'
Other examples:
> He *must* be more than fifteen: he already shaves.
>
> I *must* be late: I can see the students are already in their classrooms.

The past form of this use of *must* is *must have*:
> He *must have* lived in Italy for several years: he speaks the langugage so well.
>
> She *must have* lost her way, or she would be here by now.
>
> He *must have* been an outstanding athlete when he was young since he took part in the Olympic Games.

A sentence like:
> He *can't* earn a good salary: he lives in such a cheap house.

means: 'I am sure that he doesn't earn a good salary.'
Other examples:
> He *can't* be more than fifteen: he doesn't shave yet.
>
> I *can't* be late: I can see some students still arriving.

The past form of this use of *can't* is *can't have*:

He *can't have* lived in Italy for several years: he doesn't speak a word of the language.

She *can't have* lost her way: I saw her outside.

He *can't have* been an outstanding athlete when he was young: he has always been overweight.

EXERCISE 49

Supply *must*, *must have*, *can't*, *can't have*, as required in the following sentences:

1 He . . . be at home since he never leaves for work before this time.
2 He . . . be at home since he is always at work at this time.
3 He . . . left for work by now or he will be late.
4 He . . . left for work by now since he is always at home at this time.
5 John . . . come by bus instead of walking since he has arrived so early.
6 John . . . caught the bus since he is so late.
7 It . . . been raining during the night since the ground is so dry.
8 It . . . been raining during the night since the ground is so wet.
9 My watch . . . be wrong even though I had it repaired last week.
10 My watch . . . be wrong since I had it repaired only last week.

EXERCISE 50

Write sentences expressing the following ideas, using instead of the words *in italics* one of the following in each case: *must*, *must have*, *can't*, *can't have*.
Example: I am sure that road is three kilometres long.
    That road *must* be three kilometres long.

1 *Surely* you haven't gone on holiday with such a small sum of money.
2 *I am sure* there is a report on the football match in the newspaper.
3 The battery in that radio has run out, *I'm certain*.
4 *Surely* there is a photo in his passport.
5 *I'm sure* he isn't on the club committee: nobody would vote for him.
6 *I'm certain* he isn't over 65: he is still working.
7 *I assume* he is medically fit since he is in the army.
8 *It's obvious* the weather has been wet lately since the grass is so green.
9 *Presumably* that was Mr. Anowi who left.
10 *Surely* the cinema isn't full already.
11 *I'm certain* there is some coffee left: I bought some only yesterday.
12 *I assume* that the thieves broke in through the bedroom window.
13 *I'm sure* the servant didn't clean this room this morning.
14 She is *definitely* older than she looks.
15 *I'm sure* he succeeded because he worked so hard.
16 This is *certainly* his handwriting.
17 *Surely* she isn't his grandmother: she is far too young.
18 *I'm certain* there isn't anything but paper in this case: it is so light.

19 You *definitely* didn't wind up the clock last night: it has stopped already.
20 *I'm sure* they are brothers since they look alike.

14 'Am to' and 'am not to'

This construction is used for arrangements made for the future:

I *am to* meet my father tomorrow.

We *are to* play another match on Friday.

It can also imply an obligation, especially when used in the negative or interrogative form:

Students *are not to* borrow books from the library after next Monday.

Is he to have a medical examination before joining the college?

The usual past form of this construction is *was to, was not to* and it is for arrangements made in the past:

He *was to* travel to Nairobi by bus.

They *were to* let me know by Sunday.

EXERCISE 51

Complete the following sentences, using *am to, is to, are to, was to, were to*, as required by the sense:

1 She ... join the university last year.
2 His father ... retire next month.
3 The examination papers ... be delivered to the school last Monday.
4 The cost of electricity ... be increased soon.
5 Our windows ... be cleaned yesterday, but they weren't.
6 The next issue of the school magazine ... appear this December.
7 I ... be given another opportunity to take the examination.
8 All the windows in the dormitory ... be left open at night in future.
9 That tree ... be cut down because it would have been in the way of the proposed telephone wires.
10 The headmaster ... speak to the whole school this morning, but he was absent.

EXERCISE 52

Write ten different sentences, using the following verbs:

1 am to.	6	was not to.
2 was to.	7	were not to.
3 were to.	8	is not to.
4 is to.	9	are to.
5 am not to.	10	are not to.

15 Causative 'have' and 'get'

When we wish to indicate that something is caused to be done, we can use this structure:

We had the windows cleaned.

The verb *have* is in the tense required by the sense, and the verb for the action performed is in the past participle form:

We shall have the windows cleaned next month.

We have the windows cleaned every week.

We would have the windows cleaned if it were necessary.

A similar structure is with *get*:

We got the windows cleaned.

We shall get the windows cleaned next month.

We get the windows cleaned every week.

We would get the windows cleaned if it were necessary.

EXERCISE 53

Use the following expressions in meaningful sentences, using the tenses indicated with causative *have*:

Example: mending the roof (Future)

We shall have the roof mended tomorrow.

 1 shortening the sleeves (Future)
 2 mending these shoes (Present Simple)
 3 making a chair (Future with *going to*)
 4 cleaning this suit (Present Perfect)
 5 making a dress (Past Simple)
 6 cutting the grass (Past Perfect)
 7 cutting my hair (Past Continuous)
 8 repairing our radio (Past Simple)
 9 washing that shirt (Conditional)
10 polishing the floor (Future Perfect)
11 cleaning the board (Present Perfect)
12 darning his socks (Past Simple)
13 cutting down a tree (Future with *going to*)
14 repairing a puncture (Past Simple)
15 sweeping the floor (Present Continuous)

EXERCISE 54

Use the following expressions in meaningful sentences with causative *get* in the tenses indicated:

Example: Installing a phone (Past Simple)

We got a phone installed before we moved into that house.

 1 making a table (Future)

2 framing a picture (Past Simple)
3 checking the bill (Conditional)
4 repairing this watch (Past Perfect)
5 painting the door (Past Simple)
6 cutting down this tree (Present Continuous)
7 servicing our car (Present Simple)
8 making some coffee (Future)
9 stamping my passport (Past Simple)
10 marking this exercise (Future with *going to*)
11 building a shed (Past Simple)
12 polishing the table (Future)
13 repairing an electric lamp (Past Simple)
14 examining his eyes (Future with *going to*)
15 typing a letter (Present Continuous)

16 Clauses with 'wish'

Three different tenses can be used after the verb *wish* depending on the circumstances:

1. When we wish that something not yet happening would happen, or that something happening now would change or stop, we use the Conditional tense:

I wish you *would agree* to come.

We wish you *would tell* us the truth.

He wishes it *would stop* raining.

I wish that you *would speak* more slowly.

(Note that the Future tense cannot be used here.)

2. When we wish that a situation which does not exist did exist, or that a situation which does exist did not exist, we use the Past Simple tense:

I wish I *knew* the answer. (i.e. I don't know the answer.)

We wish we *could* help you. (i.e. We can't.)

We wish the rains *weren't* so heavy. (i.e. They are heavy.)

He wishes the terms *weren't* so long. (i.e. They are long.)

Strictly speaking, the verb here is in the Subjunctive form, but this is exactly the same as the Past Simple and does not have to be learnt separately. Note, however, that *were* is normally used instead of *was* with singular words in this construction.

She wishes she *were* married.

I wish I *were* taller.

He wishes his father *were* not so poor.

3. When we wish that something had happened which did not happen, or that something had not happened which did happen, we use the Past Perfect tense:

I wish I *had listened* to you. (i.e. I didn't.)
He wishes he *had worked* hard. (i.e. He didn't.)
I wish I *hadn't told* you. (i.e. I did.)
We wish we *hadn't come*. (i.e. We did.)

EXERCISE 55

Change the infinitives in brackets to the most suitable tense (Conditional, Past Simple or Past Perfect). It will help if you first decide which of the three groups described above, the sentence belongs to.

1 We wish you (not disturb) us yesterday evening.
2 I wish that the examination (be) further away. It starts next Thursday morning.
3 I wish it (rain) tomorrow.
4 Our teacher wishes he (choose) another profession.
5 I wish we (not have) breakfast so early this morning. I'm hungry already.
6 I wish you (stop) your dog barking. I can't listen to my radio.
7 I wish you (stop) your dog barking last night. I couldn't listen to my radio.
8 He wishes he (be) older than he is.
9 I wish he (stop) singing. I can't bear it any longer.
10 He wishes his grandfather (be) alive now.
11 He wishes his grandfather (be) alive when he won the prize: he would have been very proud of him.
12 I wish we (start) our holidays yesterday.
13 I wish I not (be) so lazy when I was in the elementary school.
14 He wishes his father (buy) him some shoes before the new term started.
15 He wishes his father (buy) him some shoes before the new term starts.
16 I wish he (go). He's been here over an hour now.
17 I wish he (give) me a lift in his car when he goes to town.
18 I wish the teacher (tell) us more about the examination before it took place.
19 She wishes he (decide) if he wants to marry her.
20 We wish we (plant) those seeds earlier last year.
21 I wish this school (have) a bigger library than it has.
22 That farmer wishes he (not sell) all his cattle. He didn't get very much for them.
23 I wish you (repeat) what you have just told me so that I don't forget.
24 I wish it (be) dry today so that we could play tennis.
25 I wish our teacher (be) more generous when he marked the examination we took last week.
26 I wish we (not arrive) late for this film. I can't follow the story.

27 I wish it (be) time to go home. I'm feeling very tired.
28 My father wishes I (choose) English as my main subject at the university, but I don't think I will.
29 I wish he (not tell) me how badly I had done. I feel very depressed now.
30 I wish I (have) more books than I have.

17 Verbs Often Confused

1. 'Been' and 'gone'

The past participle of *go* is *gone*, but when we want to imply that somebody or something has not only gone to a place but left it as well, we use *been* as a past participle.

He has *gone* to New York. (= He is there now.)
He has *been* to New York. (= He was there but is there no longer.)
Similarly with the Past Perfect:

He had already *gone* to the cinema when I called on him. (= He was at the cinema, or on his way there, when I called at his house.)
He had already *been* to the cinema when I called on him. (= He had returned from the cinema when I called on him.)

2. 'Borrow' and 'lend'

Although these two words are opposites, they are often confused. *Borrow* means *receive on loan*; *lend* means *give on loan*.

He *borrowed* some money from his friend.
The opposite process:

He *lent* some money to his friend.
(Note that we cannot say *I borrowed him some money*.)

3. 'Do' and 'make'

These two verbs have almost the same meaning and it is difficult to devise a rule to enable one to distinguish between them. Rather than rely on any rule it is wiser to learn the following expressions by heart:

do one's duty	make a mistake
do an exercise	make a request
do harm	make money
do one's best	make a living
do a favour	make the bed
do homework	make trouble
do business with	make a speech
do the housework	make a good impression
do good	make plans

do the right thing	make a statement
do without	make arrangements
do away with	make fun of (mock)
(get rid of)	make one's way
	make away with (steal)
	make a nuisance of oneself
	make progress

Note the construction *make somebody do something*. A common mistake is to use *make* with the infinitive including *to*:

The police *made* him *to confess*. WRONG

The police *made* him *confess*. RIGHT

With the passive, however, we do use *to*:

He *was made to confess* by the police.

4. 'Lie' and 'lay'

Lie (with the meanings *be in a horizontal position* or *be situated*) is intransitive and therefore has no object:

He *lies* in bed every morning till nine.

The church *lies* in a valley.

Lay is a transitive verb and therefore has an object:

That hen *lays* a lot of eggs.

The servant always *lays* the table for dinner.

Lie (with the meaning *tell an untruth*) is quite regular:

He often *lies* to his parents.

He *lied* to the headmaster.

The principal parts of these verbs are:

	Present Simple	Past Simple	Present Participle	Past Participle
lie (intr.)	*lie*	*lay*	*lying*	*lain*
lay (tr.)	*lay*	*laid*	*laying*	*laid*
lie (tell an untruth)	*lie*	*lied*	*lying*	*lied*

5. 'Lose' and 'loose'

Lose is a verb meaning the opposite of *find*:

She is afraid she might *lose* her ring.

Loose is an adjective meaning the opposite of *tight* and is connected with the verb *loosen*:

His watch was *loose* and fell off.

There is also a verb *to loose* meaning to set free (the opposite of bind)

6. 'Reach' and 'arrive'

Reach is a transitive verb and therefore must have an object:
> We *reached* London in the morning.

Arrive is intransitive and cannot have an object:
> We *arrived* in the morning.

Of course, where we arrived can be shown by using the preposition *at* or *in*:
> We *arrived in London* in the morning.

The word *there* can be used with *reach* and *arrive*:
> We *reached there* in the morning.
> We *arrived there* in the morning.

7. 'Salute' and 'greet'

Salute describes the action of raising the hand to the head in the way soldiers do when they meet a superior. (In some countries a salute is the raising of the hand in some other way.) *Greet* simply means *give greetings to* by saying *Hullo* or something similar.

> The captain *saluted* the general.
> John *greeted* his friend when he saw him in the street.

8. 'Say' and 'tell'

Rather than attempt to learn difficult and unreliable rules for the use of these two verbs, it is better to commit the following sentences to memory.

Say   He *said* nothing.
        He *said* a few words to me.
        He *said* to me, "Pass me the book."

Tell   He *told* the truth to the judge.
        He *told* him the truth.
        He *told* the judge the truth.
        He *told* me about the battle.
        He *told* me to pass the book to him.

9. 'Steal' and 'rob'

Steal is followed by the thing stolen, *rob* by a person or place. When we wish to indicate what was stolen as well as the person or place affected we use the construction *rob somebody of something*:

> He *stole* my watch.
> He *robbed* the house.
> He *robbed* me *of* my wallet.

10. 'Wear', 'put on' and 'dress'

Wear describes a state, *put on* an action. We *wear* our clothes for some hours; it takes us a short time to *put* them *on*. Both verbs are transitive and require articles of clothing, etc. as objects:

I shall *wear* my new suit to the party.

I shall *put on* a jacket when it's cooler.

Dress usually describes an action but it cannot take an article of clothing as an object:

He *is dressing* at the moment. (= He is *putting* his clothes *on*.)

It can take a person as an object:

She *is dressing* her small sister.

In a special sense it can describe the state:

She *dresses* very well. (= She wears smart clothes.)

11. 'Win' and 'beat'

Unlike *beat win* can be used intransitively:

Our team *won*.

Objects of *win* are words like *match*, *game*, *war*:

Our team *won the match*.

Beat, used in this way, has the meaning of *defeat*; it must be followed by the noun for who was beaten:

Our team *beat the champions* last week.

12. 'Wound', 'injure', 'hurt' and 'damage'

These four verbs are used in these ways:

Wound for injuries received from weapons in war and fighting

Injure for injuries received in accidents

Hurt for any injury to the body, usually minor

Damage only for objects and not for persons

Over a thousand troops were *wounded* in the battle.

Two cars collided and the passengers were *injured*.

The goal-keeper *hurt* his leg in the match.

The explosion *damaged* many shops and houses.

EXERCISE 56

Write out the following sentences using the correct words from the alternatives given:

1 If you are not more careful, you will *loose/lose* your purse.

2 When I saw him in church, he was *wearing/putting on* a blue suit.

3 The teacher told the pupil to *make/do* his homework regularly if he wanted *to make/do* progress.

4 The servant *lay/laid/lain/lied* the table.

5 The teacher *greeted/saluted* the headmaster.

6 The train *reached at/arrived at* Lagos at seven o'clock.

7 I *told/said* him to come early.

8 Our teacher always *puts on/wears* smart clothes.

9 We *laid/lied/lay/lain* the wounded man on the table.

10 We *won/beat* that school at football last week.

11 The servant was told to *make/do* the housework this morning and not forget to *do/make* the beds.

12 When the train crashed only two passengers were *wounded/injured*.

13 He *told/said* to me, ''We cannot leave tomorrow.''

14 We returned from our holidays to find that all our clothes had been *robbed/stolen*.

15 I saw the boy *make/do* away with the kitten by drowning it.

16 Although I speak English fluently, I have never *gone/been* to England.

17 Poor people are not able *to wear/put on clothes/dress* well.

18 I was *robbed of/stolen* my wallet when I was in the cinema.

19 Even though he had little money to spare he *lent/borrowed* me some.

20 He didn't know what to *tell/say*.

21 The dead man had been *laying/lying* by the side of the road for an hour.

22 In the fight both men were *injured/damaged* and some furniture was *injured/damaged/hurt*.

23 The knob on this radio set has worked *lose/loose*.

24 I think he will *make/do* a good impression at the interview.

25 Our chickens have *lied/lain/laid/lay* plenty eggs this week.

26 One of the boys in this class has *stolen/robbed* my pen.

27 Please *say/tell* me why you are late.

28 When it started to rain, he *wore/put on/dressed* his overcoat.

29 The prisoner *lay/laid/lied/lie* to the judge.

30 All the soldiers *greeted/saluted* when the king arrived.

31 Beware of that man: he is always asking to *lend/borrow* money.

32 We are going to *do/make* all the arrangements for our holidays this week.

33 By *winning/beating* that team we came second in the league.

34 He has been *dressing/wearing/putting on* that shirt for a week.

35 This notice *says/tells* there will be no bus service tomorrow.

36 The doctor told him to *loose/lose* weight.

37 His father was *injured/wounded/hurt* in the war and could no longer work.

38 He doesn't *make/do* a good living repairing shoes.

39 She has been *laying/lieing/lying* in bed all morning.

40 She *lent/borrowed* more than she could return.

41 I don't think my friend saw me because he didn't *salute/greet* me.

42 The bus *arrived/reached* my village at two in the morning.

43 I *lent/borrowed* him some money last month and he hasn't returned it yet.
44 We often *do/make* business with a Lebanese merchant.
45 I have *been/gone* to the market four times this week.
46 There is a danger that we will *lose/loose* the championship this year.
47 After lunch I will *lie/lay* down for half an hour.
48 I asked him to *do/make* me a favour.
49 I *said/told* him to give me some note-paper.
50 He *arrived/reached* earlier than I did.
51 The thieves *stole/robbed* all the jewellery.
52 He looks guilty and I think he is *lying/laying*.
53 His foolish behaviour could *make/do* him a lot of harm.
54 I *borrowed/lent* a lot of money in order to start my own business.
55 The young lady *wore/put on* a hat before entering the church.
56 We *arrived/reached* our destination at ten o'clock.
57 Did you *say/tell* that you were going to America?
58 As he was tired he *lay/lied/laid* in bed until nine o'clock.
59 Have you ever *gone/been* to America?
60 As the school has little money, we shall have to *make/do* without new exercise books this term.
61 The enemy *lay/lied/laid* down their arms last night.
62 She *said/told* she would phone in the morning.
63 Our friends *arrived/reached* in London two days ago.
64 Our headmaster always *puts on/wears* a dark tie.
65 As I have had a lot of expenses lately I have had to *lend/borrow* money.

18 Question Tags and Short Responses

1. Question Tags

In conversation we sometimes ask a question not because we need *information* but *confirmation* of what we already know. We want the person addressed to agree with us. To do this we add a *question tag* to a statement.

Expecting the answer 'yes', we say:

You like history, *don't you*?

(Affirmative statement – negative tag)

Expecting the answer 'no':

You don't like history, *do you*?

(Negative statement – affirmative tag)

The tense of the tag corresponds to the tense of the statement:

You didn't read that book, *did* you?

You were reading that book, *weren't* you?

You will read that book, *won't* you?

It will be seen from the last three examples that we repeat the auxiliary verb in the question tag. This applies to nearly all auxiliaries.

You should go there, *shouldn't* you?

He must leave early, *mustn't* he?

He could succeed, *couldn't* he?

He might have forgotten, *mightn't* he?

Exception 1: *Need* and *dare* used affirmatively in the statement are not repeated in the tag:

We need to buy a new radio, *don't* we?

He dared to stroke the lion, *didn't* he?

Exception 2: *Used to* is treated as a full verb rather than as an auxiliary:

He used to own a house, *didn't* he?

Note that there is no form *amn't I?* Instead we say *aren't I?* (*Ain't I?* is slang.)

An imperative can be made into less of a command and more of a request by the addition of an affirmative tag in the Future tense:

Pass me the sugar, *will you?*

Open the window, *will you?*

Let us leave now, *shall we?*

Finally, note that since the question tags are used almost solely in conversation the shortened, conversational form of the negative (don't, won't, hadn't, etc.) is required.

EXERCISE 57

Turn the following statements into questions by adding question tags:

1 They play football every Saturday.
2 He should write a letter.
3 He is studying French.
4 You will read his letter.
5 He doesn't live with his parents.
6 I am better at tennis than he is.
7 I am not as good at tennis as he is.
8 He collects stamps.
9 He wrote a letter last night.
10 He will visit us.
11 They often went to Lagos.
12 She must correct that work.
13 He needs a new shirt.
14 Let us play another game.
15 They used to live in Ibadan.
16 We can have the window shut.
17 His father teaches at that school.
18 He doesn't need this book.

19 He could do better if he tried.
20 Marconi didn't invent the telephone.
21 You wouldn't like a sweet.
22 The dinner is being cooked.
23 Pick up those books.
24 He mustn't come.
25 He spoke to the headmaster.
26 I must prepare for the history test.
27 The new teacher is from Kaduna.
28 Let us go to the library.
29 His uncle smokes a pipe.
30 He used to read a lot of novels.
31 He hadn't been there.
32 The interpreter was needed.
33 Let us revise the Past Perfect.
34 I should have cut the grass.
35 She visited Paris.
36 His mother used to be a nurse.
37 They ought to be sent away.
38 Switch off the light.
39 We ought to discuss the matter with him.
40 I am early.
41 He wasn't able to swim far.
42 The headmaster studied in England.
43 Let me open the window.
44 They ought to have repaired the window.
45 He doesn't have to finish the exercise.
46 Let us read a new chapter.
47 He used to be interested in biology.
48 Give me a match.
49 You had your shoes repaired.
50 The factory manager was a student at this school.

2. Short Responses

(a) To Questions Ending With Question Tags

It is normal to answer such questions briefly with a yes or no + subject + auxiliary verb. The short response echoes the question tag, i.e., the auxiliary verb is repeated in the same tense:

He has come, hasn't he? Yes, he has.
You won't come, will you? No, I won't.
He did come, didn't he? Yes, he did.
He couldn't come, could he? No, he couldn't

As was seen in the section on question tags, an affirmative statement + a negative tag expects an affirmative answer, and a negative statement + an affirmative tag expects a negative answer. However, contrary answers are, of course, possible. There are only two forms of answer:

Yes + affirmative verb   Yes, he has.
No + negative verb   No, he hasn't.

(b) To Other Questions
Questions beginning with a verb followed by a subject can also be answered briefly with a yes or no + a subject + auxiliary verb(s).

Has he finished that book? Yes, he has.
                       No, he hasn't.
Will he finish that book? Yes, he will.
                       No, he won't.
Did he finish that book?   Yes, he did.
                       No, he didn't.
Could he finish that book?   No, he couldn't.
                       Yes, he could.
Would he have finished that book? Yes,, he would have.
                       No, he wouldn't have.

Other questions of this kind begin with *who* or *which*:

Who wrote that book? Dickens did.
Who will tell us? Mary will.
Who should win the prize? John should.
Which was the best essay? His was.
Which one would be most suitable? This one would.
Which horse has won the race? That one has.

EXERCISE 58
Give short responses to the following questions:
1 He has arrived, hasn't he?
2 They came late, didn't they?
3 You did reply to that letter, didn't you?
4 You didn't check your work, did you?
5 They weren't listening, were they?
6 He wouldn't have passed, would he?
7 She could have left school last year, couldn't she?
8 It wasn't raining at nine o'clock this morning, was it?
9 He used to smoke a pipe, didn't he?
10 He would have arrived by now, wouldn't he?
11 I am doing better this year than last, aren't I?
12 He might have resigned, mightn't he?
13 You are listening to me, aren't you?
14 The meal is ready, isn't it?

15 You are going to take the examination again, aren't you?
16 Have you seen him?
17 Was she there?
18 Would he come?
19 Who found the book?
20 Did he lock the door?
21 Will you be taking part in the play?
22 Were they eating when you arrived?
23 Who filled in this form?
24 Had he been to England before he came here?
25 Was the door open when you arrived?
26 Did they get married last year?
27 Which dictionary is more reliable?
28 Is it still raining?
29 Which teacher gave you this book?
30 Wouldn't he have agreed with me?

2 Indirect Speech

In changing from the actual words of the speaker (direct speech) to words we use to report what has been said (indirect or reported speech) there are certain rules we have to pay attention to.

1 Tense Changes

> "I have studied French for three years," he said.
> He said he had studied French for three years.

Providing the reporting verb (in the above example *said*) is in a Past Tense, the tenses of the speech are normally changed. If the reporting verb is in any of the other tenses, no changes are made in the tenses of the speech.

The tense changes are as follows:

Present Simple becomes Past Simple:
> "I study French every evening," he said.
> He said he studied French every evening.

Present Continuous becomes Past Continuous:
> "I am studying French at the moment," he said.
> He said he was studying French at the moment.

Present Perfect becomes Past Perfect:
> "I have studied French for three years," he said.
> He said he had studied French for three years.

Present Perfect Continuous becomes Past Perfect Continuous:
> "I have been studying French for three years," he said.
> He said he had been studying French for three years.

Past Simple usually changes to Past Perfect.
> "I studied French last year," he said.
> He said he had studied French last year.

Past Continuous can remain Past Continuous or become Past Perfect Continuous:

"I was studying French last year," he said.

He said he was studying French last year.

He said he had been studying French last year.

Future becomes Conditional:

"I shall study French next year," he said.

He said he would study French next year.

Future Perfect becomes Conditional Perfect:

"I shall have studied French for three years next October," he said.

He said he would have studied French for three years next October.

(The Conditional and the Past Perfect are not normally changed.)

Note 1: When the reporting verb *say* takes an indirect object it is changed to *tell* before indirect speech:

"We shall go on holiday at the end of June," he said to me.

He told me they would go on holiday at the end of June.

Note 2: If it is felt that what was said is still true when it is reported, we can keep the tense of the original speech. This is particularly common when we are reporting scientific facts:

"Water boils at 100 °C," the teacher said.

The teacher said that water boils at 100 °C.

2 Pronoun and Possessive Adjective Changes

"I have left *my* book in *your* car," Mary told her brother.

Mary told her brother that she had left *her* book in *his* car.

In making such changes it is wiser to rely on the sense than to attempt to apply rules.

3 Demonstrative Adjective Changes

"I borrowed *this* pen from my brother," John said.

John said that he borrowed *that* pen from his brother.

John said that he borrowed *the* pen from his brother.

The changes are simply:

Direct	Indirect
this	that *or* the
these	those *or* the

4 Adverb Changes

"I'll bring you the photo *tomorrow*," he said.

He said he would bring the photo *the next day*.

Such a change is only made, of course, if the speech is reported on a day other than when it is made. Bearing this point in mind, we *usually* make the following changes:

Direct	*Indirect*
today	that day
yesterday	the day before, the previous day
tomorrow	the next day, the following day
yesterday morning	the morning before, the previous morning
yesterday afternoon	the afternoon before, the previous afternoon
yesterday evening	the evening before, the previous evening
last night	the night before, the previous night
here	there
ago	before
now	then

5 Commands

"*Take* the books to the office," the clerk said to me.

The clerk told me *to take* the books to the office.

Note that in addition to the usual changes the imperative form of the verb was changed to the infinitive.

6 Questions

"Why have you locked the door?" the teacher asked me.

The teacher asked me why I had locked the door.

"Have you been to Lagos before?" my father asked him.

My father asked him if he had been to Lagos before.

To change a question from direct to indirect speech:

(a) the statement order (subject + verb) is used instead of the question order (verb + subject);

(b) the question mark is dropped;

(c) questions not beginning with an interrogative word like *why*, *who*, *when*, *what*, require the addition of *if* or *whether*.

(Either *if* or *whether* can generally be used but it is preferable to use *whether* when *or* occurs in the speech. For example: The waiter asked *whether* I would have tea or coffee.)

7 Exclamations

In order to express an exclamation in indirect speech it is necessary to use an expression which will give the idea of the original:

"Never! I will never agree to such a proposal," he said.

He said he would *absolutely* never agree to such a proposal.

"Good gracious! I have never heard of such a thing," he said.

He *was very surprised* and said he had never heard of such a thing.

8 Speeches Containing not only Statements

"I am going to Nairobi. Have you ever been there?"

He said he was going to Nairobi and asked if I had ever been there.

If a speech contains not only a statement but also a question, or a command, or an exclamation, more than one reporting verb will be necessary in the indirect form.

9 'Yes' and 'no'

"Yes, I'll come and see you soon," he said.

He said he would come and see me soon.

When occurring at the beginning of a sentence of direct speech, *yes* and *no* can be omitted in the indirect form.

"Have you ever seen a plane crash?" he asked. "No," I replied.

He asked me if I had ever seen a plane crash and I said I had not.

"I don't think there will be any more rain today. Do you?" I said. "No," she replied.

I said I didn't think there would be any more rain that day and asked her what she thought. She agreed with me.

When *yes* or *no* stand alone they are changed in indirect speech to a phrase echoing the main verb, or a word like *agree*, *disagree* can be used.

Avoid using the expression *in the negative* and *in the affirmative*, except in very formal style.

10 'Must'

It is essential to distinguish between the three uses of *must*:

(i) *Must* used for the actual present in direct speech becomes *had to* in indirect speech:

"I *must* write to my father," he said.

He said he *had to* write to his father.

(ii) *Must* used for the future in direct speech becomes *would have to* in indirect speech:

"I *must* leave for England next week," he said.

He said he *would have to leave* for England the following week.

(iii) *Must* used for a rule that always applies in direct speech remains *must* in indirect speech:

"Children *must* obey their parents," he said.

He said that children *must* obey their parents.

(iv) *Must* implying certainty (see pages 49–50) does not change:

"Obaro must be over seventeen since he's already at university," she said.

She said that Obaro must be over seventeen since he was already at university.

EXERCISE 59

Write in indirect speech form, using the introductory words suggested and any others necessary:

1 "They have been living in Jos since 1960 and they will probably remain there for many years." My brother told me . . .

2 "When we arrive in Lagos and meet my uncle, I'll give you the money you lent me last week." He said that when we . . .

3 "Anybody who finds the ring and hands it in at a police station will be rewarded." The notice said that . . .

4 "We shall arrive home before six if the bus doesn't break down." The driver said that we . . . .

5 "We would have played football with you last Saturday if it hadn't rained." I told the captain of the other team . . . (Reported three weeks later)

6 "You must finish your compositions before the end of the lesson as I am going to mark them this evening." The teacher told us we . . . (Reported next day)

7 "The coffee crop has been much better this year and our earnings from exports will enable us to expand our home industries." The Minister told the conference that our . . . (Reported two years later)

8 "Did you watch television last night?" My friend asked me . . . (Reported a week later)

9 "Having spent only a few days in the country, I can give you only very general impressions." The tourist told me . . .

10 "Have you ever been told that you must always copy carefully?" The teacher asked the students . . .

11 "Can you tell me the way to St. Mary's Church? I have been trying to find it for over half an hour." A stranger asked me . . .

12 "Can I help you with your homework? You seem to be having difficulties." My father asked me ...

13 "Have you read Graham Greene's latest novel? You should try to get it from the library." My English teacher asked me ...

14 "Shall we have time to finish this exercise before the end of the lesson? Some of the questions are quite difficult and we have to think about them." I asked the maths teacher ...

15 "Please give me your pen as soon as you have finished writing. Mine has run dry." I asked a boy ...

16 "Good heavens! What are we to do now that the electricity has failed?" Somebody ...

17 "Did anyone telephone while I was out? I hope you took the message if they did." The Director asked his secretary ...

18 "I called to see you at five o'clock, but you weren't home. I thought you were always in at that time." John told his aunt ...

19 "Did you visit Norway while you were studying in Europe? I have always wanted to visit that country." Mr. Jones asked my brother ...

20 "Did you use a dictionary when you were writing this essay? I don't think you did. If you had, you would not have made all these mistakes." My teacher asked me ...

21 "Did your father go to secondary school?" "No." My headmaster asked me ...

22 "Can we use a pencil or do we have to use a ballpoint? I have forgotten to bring my ballpoint." A student asked if ...

23 "Does the bus arrive before nine?" "Yes, I think it does." Somebody asked me ...

24 "Would you lend me your grammar book?" "Good gracious, no. You haven't returned a book I lent you six months ago." He asked me ...

3 Articles and Words of Quantity

1 Countable and Uncountable Nouns

There is a useful distinction that can be made between countable and uncountable nouns. It helps us to know when to use the articles, the plural form, much, many, some, any and other words of quantity. Although it is very difficult to decide which nouns are countable and which uncountable by applying rules, nouns for materials (*wood*, *glass*, *meat*, etc.) and for liquids (*water*, *milk*, *juice*, etc.) are usually uncountable as are abstract nouns (*bravery*, *joy*, *truth*, etc.)

Here are lists of countable and uncountable nouns:

Countable		Uncountable	
match	toy	water	electricity
box	bicycle	oil	happiness
goat	poem	dust	poetry
table	river	weather	darkness
bowl	scene	air	scenery
curtain	dentist	paper	dentistry
rule	bottle	food	mercy
book	knife	fruit	intelligence
shoe	lamp	mud	honesty
needle	telephone	wool	carefulness

Normally, uncountable nouns are not found in the plural form, and it is not possible to express the singular of uncountable nouns. But we can place a suitable countable noun before the uncountable as is shown in the following examples of the most common nouns used in this way:

soap	a bar of soap
furniture	a piece of furniture
news	an item of news

equipment	a piece of equipment
grass	a blade of grass
dust	a speck of dust
sand	a grain of sand
salt	a grain of salt
advice	a piece of advice
lightning	a flash of lightning
jewellery	a piece of jewellery
clothing	an article of clothing
sunshine	a ray of sunshine
land	a plot of land
glass	a sheet of glass
chalk	a piece of chalk
bread	a slice, a loaf of bread
information	a piece of information

Some words can be countable or uncountable according to the context in which they are used. Examples are:

	Uncountable	Countable
air	*the oxygen and nitrogen around us*	*tune*
change	*money in small coins given for large or foreign money*	*alteration*
coffee	*the plant, the drink*	*a cup of coffee*
dress	*clothing*	*a frock*
fire	*the general word for combustion*	*a single occurrence of fire*
glass	*the material made of sand, potash, etc.*	*a drinking vessel made of glass (Also: glasses = spectacles)*
hair	*all the strands together*	*one strand by itself*
instruction	*teaching*	*an order*
iron	*the metal*	*a tool for smoothing clothes*
land	*area of ground*	*a country*
light	*opposite of darkness*	*the fire given by a match; lamp, torch, candle*
paper	*the material*	*a learned article, a newspaper*
property	*belongings*	*a house or area of land, a characteristic*
room	*space*	*part of a house enclosed by walls*
rubber	*the substance*	*a piece of rubber for erasing*
speech	*the power of speaking*	*spoken words*
stone	*the material*	*a pebble*
tea	*the plant, the drink*	*a cup of tea, a tea party*

wood	*the material*	*a small forest*
work	*effort for a purpose*	*a piece of literary, artistic, or musical composition*
youth	*period of being young*	*a young man*

2 The Definite Article

1. *The definite article ('the') is used:*

(a) When the noun is known (to the reader or hearer)

   The letter he received was posted on Friday.

The words 'he received' tell us which letter is referred to. Often a person or thing is known because it is the only one:

   The sun is millions of kilometres away.

Or the reader or hearer knows which one is referred to:

   Give me *the* book. (i.e. the book we are talking about, which you borrowed, etc.)

   The shop closes at six. (i.e. the one we are in, where I work, which we are going to this afternoon, etc.)

If the person or thing were not known, we would, of course, use the indefinite article:

   A book is on the table.

(b) Before oceans, seas, rivers, deserts:

   the Pacific   *the* Sahara
   the Baltic   *the* Nile

When the name of a country consists of an adjective + noun, the definite article is required unless the adjective is: North, South, East, West, Upper, Lower, Great or New.

   the United Kingdom   **but** North Korea
   the United Arab Republic   West Germany
   the Soviet Union   Upper Volta
               Great Britain
               New Zealand

Four countries with one-word names can take the definite article:

   the Lebanon   *the* Argentine
   the Congo   *the* Sudan

The Netherlands always takes the definite article.

Note also: *the* North Pole, *the* South Pole.

Hotels, cinemas, theatres and ships also require the definite article:

   He is staying at *the* National Hotel.

   We went to *the* Odeon last night.

   He crossed the Atlantic in *the* Queen Elizabeth II.

(c) Proper nouns used in the plural require the definite article:

    the Alps
    the Philippines
    the Russells

(d) Before superlatives

    Of all the girls in the class she is *the* most intelligent.
    He told me *the* latest news.

The definite article is not used before a superlative when the condition of the same person or thing at different times is compared:

    We are busiest in summer.

Note that when the word *most* is used in the sense of *very* or *the majority* it is not a superlative and does not require the definite article:

    I find his book most interesting.
    I have read most of the books you gave me.

(e) Before an adjective used as a noun to give the meaning 'all the':

    The poor were helped by *the* rich.
    The young have to support *the* old.

(f) Before comparatives in constructions like:

    The more it rains, *the* worse the roads will be.
    The older he gets, *the* more difficult it is for him to find a job.

Such constructions show a parallel increase or decrease.

    The definite article is also used before the comparative adjective when a noun would normally take the definite article is understood to follow:

    He is *the* younger of the two boys.
    Of the two radios this is *the* more expensive.

(g) Before certain expressions of time:

    in *the* morning, afternoon, evening, night
    on *the* previous day, *the* day before
    on *the* following day, *the* day after
    the previous morning, afternoon, evening, night
    the next morning, afternoon, evening, night
    the week before last, *the* week after next

But the following expressions of time do not take the definite article:

    last week, month, year
    next week, month, year
    midnight, midday, noon

(h) Before musical instruments:

    She plays *the* guitar.
    (But not with games: He plays football.)

(i) In scientific writing we can use *the* before a countable noun in the singular

to refer to a whole class:

> *The* elephant lives longer than most animals.
>
> *The* atomic bomb was invented in 1944.

2. *The definite article is omitted:*

(a) Before plural nouns used for a whole class:
> Snakes are often dangerous.
>
> Bicycles cost more than they used to.

(b) Before uncountable nouns with a general meaning:
> Meat contains protein.
>
> Paper is produced from wood.
>
> He studied history.

Abstract nouns belong to this category:

> Honesty is the best policy.
>
> Generosity was one of his virtues.

If an uncountable noun is defined, it ceases to have a general meaning and therefore takes the definite article:

> The meat we bought yesterday has gone bad.
>
> The paper produced in Norway is of high quality.
>
> He studied the history of Europe.
>
> The honesty of the Sudanese is well known.
>
> The generosity he has shown us is surprising.

(c) Before the names of languages used as nouns:
> He learnt Russian.
>
> My brother studied Swahili.

If the word for the language is used as an adjective, the definitive article is necessary:

> The Russian language is spoken by millions of people.
>
> He thought there was a great future for the Swahili language.

(d) Before 'man' used in the sense of 'mankind':
> Man has more intelligence than the other animals.

(e) In expressions for means of travel used generally:

by rail	by bus	by road	by air
by train	by sea	by car	

When we are more specific the article is required:

> He travelled by *the* 8 o'clock train.

In certain other expressions:

at home	on top	on foot	on loan

There is a slight difference in meaning between the two sentences:

> He has gone to church.
>
> He has gone to the church.

In the first sentence we imply that he has go to church for the usual purpose one goes to church, namely, to worship; in the second that he has gone there for some other purpose — possibly to do a job. Similarly with *school*:

Some students didn't come to school this morning.

My father came to the school to talk to the headmaster.

Other common words of this kind are: *college, university, hospital, market, prison.*

Compare: My brother is in hospital (i.e. he is ill).

My sister, who is a nurse, is at *the* hospital.

The criminal is now in prison.

The warder lives in *the* prison.

EXERCISE 60

Insert the definite article where required in the following sentences:

1 ... shopkeepers have to work ... longer hours than ... teachers.

2 ... aeroplane is ... fastest means of transport.

3 ... language spoken in Algeria is ... Arabic.

4 Our grandmother is coming to visit us ... next month.

5 ... trees we planted ... last year have nearly all died.

6 She was overcome by ... beauty of ... scenery.

7 ... biology teacher told us that several books have been written about ... bee.

8 He studied ... languages when he was in ... North America.

9 It was on ... fourth of ... month that he arrived.

10 ... longer he stays in ... capital, ... more money he spends.

11 He flew across ... Mediterranean and landed in ... south of France.

12 ... wounded were taken to ... new hospital.

13 ... Congo has one of ... heaviest rainfalls of ... Africa.

14 ... tortoise lives longer than ... most animals.

15 ... oil is vital to ... economy of many countries.

16 Some people doubt if ... man will ever be able to avoid ... war.

17 ... Amazon is one of ... longest rivers in ... world.

18 My brother first went to ... school when he was five and he joined ... secondary school in this town ... last year.

19 ... English language has been influenced by ... Latin.

20 ... Canaries are islands belonging to Spain.

21 ... houses built of ... mud cost much less than those built of ... brick.

22 ... earlier everybody arrives, ... sooner we can start.

23 ... camel is able to go without ... water for several weeks.

24 ... most interesting book I have ever read was about ... travel in ... South America.

25 On ... last occasion he stayed in this town he went to ... cheapest hotel.

26 ... enthusiasm he showed for his job earned him ... salary increase he was

granted ... last month.

27 ... apples contain ... vitamins.

28 ... telephone has improved ... communications more than any other invention.

29 ... foundations of ... new school are made of ... iron and ... concrete.

30 Five delegates from ... United States and two from ... West Germany attended ... conference in ... South America.

31 ... lazy students all over ... world often find ... examinations difficult.

32 ... book he was reading was on ... loan from ... library.

33 ... mosquitoes which bit him may have been ... carriers of ... malaria.

34 When he joined ... army, he was ... youngest man in ... regiment.

35 ... rainy season started early this year and ... harvest will probably be ... best we have had for ... last few years.

36 ... Atlantic is one of ... roughest oceans in ... world.

37 Reading ... English magazines is one of ... best ways of improving your knowledge of ... language.

38 He has been given a scholarship by ... British Council and will go to ... United Kingdom as soon as he gets a visa from ... Passport Office.

39 ... dress she was wearing last night was made of ... silk.

40 ... oxygen is essential for ... life.

41 ... ants have made no progress at all while ... man has evolved rapidly.

42 ... tobacco is known to be ... cause of ... many diseases.

43 ... writers and ... artists are not usually among ... best paid members of ... society.

44 ... cat belongs to ... same family as ... lion.

45 ... Pyrenees divide ... France from ... Spain.

46 In ... Second World War ... economy of many countries was upset.

47 ... nuclear energy is now used for generating ... electricity.

48 ... Arabic spoken in Egypt is not ... same as ... Arabic spoken in Iraq.

49 ... Everest, which is in ... Himalayas, was first climbed in 1953.

50 My uncle arrived by ... rail ... last night.

51 She is ... taller of my two sisters but she is not ... taller than I am.

52 ... President went to ... conference by ... air ... day before yesterday.

53 ... criminal was sent to ... prison for five years.

54 ... Prime Minister will visit ... Soviet Union ... next month.

55 ... drinking of ... alcohol is forbidden in ... Saudi Arabia.

56 ... causes of ... last world war are still disputed.

57 ... exhibition of ... paintings in ... Municipal Hall was opened by ... Minister of Education ... day before yesterday.

58 ... illiteracy is still ... one of ... great problems in ... world.

59 I had lunch at ... restaurant near ... river ... yesterday afternoon.

60 ... African sculpture is now well known in most of ... countries of ... Europe.

3 The Indefinite Article

The indefinite article is *a* or *an*. *A* is used before consonants, *an* before words beginning with a vowel:

> an apple   an order   an interesting book.

If the first letter of a word is an unpronounced *h* it is treated as a vowel for this purpose:

> an hour   an heir   an honour   an honest man.

Some words begin with a vowel but are pronounced as if they begin with a *y* and are therefore preceded by *a*:

> a university   a European   a useful hint

1. *The indefinite article is used:*

(a) Before singular countable nouns when we are not referring to something or someone specific or when the reader does not know which one is referred to:

> *A* parcel arrived for you this morning.
> *A* friend of yours called for you.

(b) In the sense of 'one':

> I read *a* book every week last term.
> I gave him *a* dollar for the work.
> (Also before hundred, thousand, million, billion, etc., when used in the singular as an alternative to *one*:
> We travelled *a* hundred kilometres before midday.)

(c) With the meaning 'each':

> Last week the secretary wrote ten letters *a* day.
> His salary has been increased by a hundred pounds *a* year.

(d) With the names of occupations:

> His father is *a* doctor.
> She wants to become *a* nurse.

(e) When we imply that a person, whose name we use with a title, is unknown to us:

> *A* Mr. Nwosu wishes to speak to you.
> *A* Miss Okigbo has applied for the post.

(f) With an adjective followed by 'one':

> He looked at several coats and chose *a grey one*.
> He glanced over some exercises and did *an easy one*.

Note the following points:

(i) The indefinite article follows *such*:

> It is *such a* hot day he can't work.
> He was making *such a* noise that I couldn't hear the radio.

(ii) The indefinite article follows the adjective if the adjective is preceded by *too*:

He is *too wise a* man to get involved in an argument.

It is *too long an* exercise for us to do today.

The indefinite article may come before or after *rather* used with an adjective:

It is *a rather hot* day.

or: It is *rather a hot* day.

The indefinite article changes the meaning when used before *few* and *little*:

I have *few* books. (= I haven't as many books as I'd like to have.)

I have *a few* books. (= I haven't many books but I have some and I'm not complaining.)

There was *little* rain last month. (= There wasn't much rain last month.)

There was *a little* rain last month. (=· There was some rain last month.)

(*Few* and *little* are often expressed *very few*, *very little*:

I have *very few* books.

There was *very little* rain last month.)

2. *The indefinite article is not used:*

(a) *When the noun is uncountable:*

My new desk is made of *steel*.

He gave up drinking *coffee*.

But it is used before uncountable nouns when we imply a comparison between an uncountable noun and others of the same kind:

A cloth of this quality is very expensive.

A purer water than this does not exist.

(b) *When the noun is the name of a meal:*

We had *breakfast* at seven o'clock.

I had *dinner* before going out.

If, however, we use the name of a meal in the sense of a party, the indefinite article is required:

There is going to be *a* dinner for the old boys of the school next week.

(c) *When the noun is plural.*

EXERCISE 61

Insert *a* or *an* where necessary in the gaps in the following sentences:

1 The shirt he is wearing today is made of ... nylon, but he prefers ... cotton ones.

2 I like to spend ... evening listening to ... music, but my sister prefers going to see ... play.

3 He spent ... lot of money on ... presents for his family last year.

4 One of the men was wearing ... evening dress.

5 I prefer ... fish to ... meat.

6 Not many people read ... poetry, but quite ... few read ... novels.

7 Please pass me ... rubber. I have made ... mistake.

8 ... factory needs ... modern machinery if it is to produce ... good quality materials.

9 One does not have to be ... scientist to know that ... oil will not mix with ... water.

10 He bought ... iron and pressed ... pair of trousers every day.

11 She was wearing ... silver bracelet, but her necklace was made of ... gold.

12 When ... cigarettes went up in ... price he bought ... pipe and smoked ... tobacco.

13 ... glass, unlike ... water, is ... poor conductor of ... electricity.

14 ... fire destroys ... vast amounts of ... property every year. ... sensible person protects himself by having ... insurance policy.

15 He has ... glass of ... fruit juice before ... breakfast every morning.

16 She bought ... newspaper and ... magazine to read as she was going on ... long journey.

17 ... ebony is ... very hard wood; balsa is such ... soft wood that it can easily be cut with ... razor blade.

18 Balzac was ... outstanding French novelist who produced ... large number of studies of ... human nature.

19 In some countries ... carpentry is not ... occupation for ... girl.

20 ... people who have ... little patience rarely succeed.

21 ... university will be started in this town when ... permission is obtained from the Government.

22 She did not like being ... nurse and trained to become ... teacher.

23 She has ... plenty of clothes but ... few shoes.

24 He reads two newspapers ... day when he is at ... home.

25 It would be ... honour to be invited to stay with ... such ... distinguished ... person.

26 When he was ... librarian in Nigeria he had ... much higher salary that he has now as ... teacher in this country.

27 He is always complaining that he has ... few clothes.

28 He bought ... belt made of ... leather since his old one, which was made of ... plastic, had worn out.

29 He waited ... such ... long ... time for ... reward that he thought there was ... little hope of ever receiving one.

30 Last term we had to write ... essay ... week for our history teacher.

EXERCISE 62

Insert *a*, *an* or *the* where necessary in the gaps in the following passage:

... day before yesterday I went shopping. There is ... bus which goes from near my house to ... main market of ... town, but as I was not in ... hurry, I went on ... foot. On ... way ... small boy tried to sell me ... magazine, but as he didn't have ... change, I couldn't buy it.

... first shop I went to was ... butcher's. There are over twenty butchers in our town, but now I always go to ... same one. His prices are ... lower than anywhere else, and ... quality of his meat is ... higher. ... Last year I tried several others but I found ... few could compete with him. In this shop I bought ... kilo of beef and ... chicken.

I next went to buy ... packet of ... cigarettes. I don't smoke myself, but my brother does and he likes ... most expensive ones available ... older he gets ... more extravagant he becomes. I have often advised him to give up ... smoking as ... tobacco is dangerous, but he goes on smoking ... packet of cigarettes ... day.

Then I went and bought ... vegetables we needed for ... coming week. ... owner of ... shop I went to is ... old friend of mine and gives me ... bigger reductions than any other greengrocer. He invited me into his room at ... back of ... shop and offered me ... cup of ... coffee. We talked about ... latest news; there had been ... earthquake in ... Congo and he was ... most concerned because ... relation of his was working in ... area as ... doctor. ... earthquake had destroyed two hospitals.

After we had chatted for ... few minutes, I went home and had ... lunch with my family.

4 'Some' and 'Any'

These two words are used to describe an indefinite number or quantity.

'Some' is used:

1. In most affirmative sentences:
     There were *some* iron filings near the magnet.
     The teacher put *some* water in the glass.

2. In questions expecting the answer 'yes':
     Would you like *some* coffee?
     Have you *some* money to spare?

3. With the meaning *not all*:
     Some people like travelling.
     Some traders make a lot of money.

'Any' is used:

1. In negative sentences:
     There weren't *any* iron filings near the magnet.
     The teacher didn't put *any* water in the glass.

2. In questions to which the answer is as likely to be 'yes' as 'no':

Were there *any* iron filings near the magnet?
Did the teacher put *any* water in the glass?

3. In conditional clauses:
   If there were *any* iron filings near the magnet, they would have been attracted to it.
   If the teacher had put *any* water in the glass, it would have changed colour.

4. With the meaning *no matter which*:
   Buy *any* cigarettes you like.
   Send *any* student to get the books.

Note: We usually make *any* negative by using *no* after the verbs *be* and *have*. *It is quite wrong to use 'no any'.*

   There are *no* students here who took the exam last year.
   She has *no* money.

In speech the form *-n't any* is normal after *be* and *have*:

   There *aren't any* students here who took the exam last year.
   She *hasn't any* money.

The usual form with other verbs is *not* + verb + *any*:

   He did *not* buy *any* books.
   We did *not* kill *any* animals.
   She will *not* give *any* reason.

EXERCISE 63

Supply *some* or *any* as necessary in the following sentences:

 1 He hasn't ... ink left.
 2 Have you met ... foreigners in your town?
 3 He gave me ... book I asked for.
 4 He didn't give me ... news.
 5 Do you want ... soup? (Expecting the answer 'yes')
 6 I hope there won't be ... rain tomorrow.
 7 ... artists are poor men.
 8 Write a composition of ... length you like.
 9 He didn't have ... sleep last night.
10 Has he read ... novels this term?
11 He was unable to give us ... advice.
12 We didn't study ... algebra last year.
13 ... of the glasses were broken.
14 We had ... money but not enough.
15 She hasn't ... children.
16 ... of the work was completed by ten o'clock.
17 ... Nigerian pilgrims cross the Sudan.
18 He asked if I had seen ... films this month.

19 He got ... sleep on the journey but I didn't get ...
20 I will accept ... novels you can let me have.
21 ... languages are much more difficult than English.
22 ... cigarettes have filter tips.
23 He couldn't find ... book on the subject.
24 If there are ... latecomers they won't be admitted.
25 There isn't ... furniture in that room.
26 ... dictionaries are useless.
27 Please buy ... milk this morning. We have hardly ... left.
28 That question is so easy that ... student could answer it.
29 Is there ... coffee left in the tin? There ought to be.
30 I haven't ... time to spare for the next week.

EXERCISE 64
1 Write five sentences using *some* in affirmative sentences.
2 Write five sentences using *some* in questions expecting the answer 'yes'.
3 Write five sentences using *some* with the meaning *not all*.
4 Write five sentences using *any* in negative sentences.
5 Write five sentences using *any* in questions.
6 Write five sentences using *any* in conditional sentences.
7 Write five sentences using *any* with the meaning *no matter which*.

EXERCISE 65
Supply *a*, *an*, or *some* where necessary in the following sentences:
 1 I bought ... cigarettes but I didn't buy ... tobacco.
 2 ... houses in this town are made of ... brick and others are made of ... wood.
 3 I've read ... books on science in the last month.
 4 ... people have ... great liking for ... hot food.
 5 He gave me ... foreign coins for my collection.
 6 There is ... envelope and ... writing-paper in ... drawer of that desk.
 7 There has been ... sunshine today but not much.
 8 In ... countries ... child under the age of sixteen is not allowed to marry.
 9 ... plays by Shakespeare are tragedies.
10 There is only ... little ink left in this pen and I have ... more letters to write.
11 She will have to buy ... new clothes and ... pair of shoes before the new term starts.
12 There is ... little hope of success now that you have wasted ... so much ... time.
13 ... poetry is ... art.
14 ... trees are valuable because their trunks can be used as ... telegraph poles.
15 ... clubs had to close because ... few boys were interested.

16 I bought ... interesting books in ... shop near the church.

17 ... seeds I planted last year never germinated but ... few did.

18 He was able to give ... little time to his family since he had ... such ... lot of work to do.

19 ... teachers take ... interest in their pupils while others don't.

20 If you find ... shop open, buy ... bread and ... carton of ... milk.

5 'Much', 'Many' and Similar Words

The distinction between countable and uncountable nouns is useful in enabling us to decide whether to use *much* or *many*. *Much* is used before uncountable, *many* before countable nouns:

much oil   *much* water   *much* food

many rivers   *many* pens   *many* clocks

However, an expression of quantity or number like *a lot of* is often more normal usage, particularly in spoken language, than *much* or *many*:

He drinks *a lot of* milk. (rather than *much* milk)

I gave him *a lot of* postage stamps. (rather than *many* postage stamps.)

The use of *much* and *many* is normally restricted to:

(a) Negative statements:

There isn't *much* salt left.

I haven't seen *many* films lately.

(b) Questions:

Does *much* rain fall in July?

Are there *many* snakes in this country?

But questions expecting the answer 'yes' usually require one of the expressions of quantity or number:

Hasn't the price of *a lot of* things gone up lately?

(c) Expressions with *so, too, as* and *how*:

I have done *so much* work I'm exhausted.

He ate *too much* rice.

I have *as much* money as he has.

He told me *how many* brothers he had.

Plenty of is another expression often used in this way before either countables and uncountables. *A great deal of, a great quantity of* are used before uncountables, and *a large number of, a great many* before countables. Similarly *a long way* is used in place of *far*.

There are *plenty of* restaurants in this town.

The country sold *a great deal of* coffee last month.

Ethiopia exports *a great quantity of* coffee.

The President shook hands with *a large number of* people at the reception.

A *great many* questions remained to be answered.

He travelled *a long way* for the interview.

EXERCISE 66

Supply *much*, *many* or other suitable expressions of quantity or number in the gaps in the following sentences:

1 Has the carpenter made ... chairs this week?
2 He didn't buy ... food as he was going away.
3 He read ... history when he was young.
4 I didn't earn ... money last summer.
5 That author has written ... books.
6 We have ... time to spare this week. .
7 He didn't have ... sleep last night.
8 He used to eat ... apples.
9 We didn't study ... poems last year.
10 Were there ... students at the debate?
11 There are ... rose bushes in his garden.
12 My uncle has ... money.
13 He hasn't as ... friends as he used to have.
14 Did the postman bring ... letters?
15 There was ... water on the grass.
16 There aren't ... people who would agree with you.
17 The librarian has ordered ... books for the school library.
18 So ... people applied for that post that I don't think I'll get it.
19 We haven't ... more exercises to do.
20 He made ... notes on the subject.

6 'Too' and 'Enough'

'Too'

Look at these examples:

He is *too* young to go to school.

This coat is *too* big for me.

It is *too* wet for us to play football.

In each of the above sentences the adjective after *too* is followed by the idea, expressed or understood, that something is impossible or undesirable, i.e. by a negative idea.

If *too* is preceded by a negative verb, then the following idea is positive:

He *isn't too* young to go to school.

(i.e. He can go to school.)

Note that the construction after the adjective (or adverb) following *too* is

one of the following: the infinitive with to; for + noun or pronoun; or for +
noun or pronoun + the infinitive with to.

EXERCISE 67
Combine the following pairs of sentences, using *too* in place of *very*:
Example: That book is very difficult. It is not suitable for first year students.
        That book is too difficult for first year students.
 1 That bicycle is very expensive. I can't buy it.
 2 This box is very heavy. I can't carry it.
 3 The water in the tank is very dirty. We can't drink it.
 4 He is very stupid. He can't pass the simplest exam.
 5 That road is very narrow. The bus can't go along it.
 6 The rent of that house is very high. We can't pay it.
 7 The town is very far away. We can't walk there.
 8 He is very short. He can't become a policeman.
 9 The exercise was very long. I couldn't finish it.
10 The road is very muddy. We won't be able to drive to the village.
11 He is very poor. He can't stay at school.
12 His handwriting is very untidy. I can't read it.
13 She was very young. She wasn't allowed to get married.
14 The light from this torch is very faint. We can't see our way.
15 The ground was very stony. The plants wouldn't grow.

'Enough'

Look at these examples:
        He is old *enough* to go to school.
        This coat is big *enough* for me.
        It is dry *enough* for us to play football.
    In these sentences the word *enough* is followed by the idea that something is
possible or desirable, i.e. by a positive idea.
    If *enough* is preceded by a negative verb, then the following idea is
negative:
        He *isn't* old *enough* to go to school.
        (i.e. He can't go to school.)
    Note that *enough* always follows the adjective or adverb.
    Possible constructions after *enough* are the same as those after an adjective
(adverb) + *too*: the infinitive with to; for + noun or pronoun; for + noun or
pronoun + the infinitive with to.

EXERCISE 68
Combine the following pairs of sentences, using *enough*:
Example: She knows some English. She understands what I said.
        She knows enough English to understand what I said.

1 There is some ink in this bottle. I shall be able to fill my pen.
2 His exam results were quite good. He was promoted.
3 I bought some cloth. It will make two shirts.
4 His mother is strong. She is able to do the work of a man.
5 He is quite clever. He will go to the university.
6 These oranges aren't ripe. We can't eat them.
7 He speaks French very well. He could pass as a Frenchman.
8 It was still light. We were able to finish the game.
9 The passage was short. We were able to study it in one lesson.
10 I borrowed some money. I was then able to pay the bill.
11 He didn't have the book long. He wasn't able to read it.
12 There was some food in the store. We all had something to eat.
13 The water was deep. We were able to swim in it.
14 He went to school for some time. He learnt to read and write.
15 The trousers he was wearing were long. They could have been worn by his elder brother.

EXERCISE 69
Rewrite the following sentences, using *too* or *enough* according to the sense:
Example: My brother is quite strong and can lift a piano alone.
   My brother is strong enough to lift a piano alone.
   The bread was so stale that we couldn't eat it.
   The bread was too stale for us to eat.
1 He has made so many mistakes that he won't pass the exam.
2 His desk is so untidy he can't work at it.
3 I arrived so late that I didn't catch the train.
4 The dog barked loudly and frightened the burglars.
5 He was very foolish and agreed to the high price the trader demanded.
6 He is now quite old and could retire.
7 The coffee I was given was so hot that I couldn't drink it.
8 That book is so dear I can't afford to buy it.
9 He saved up some money and bought a bicycle.
10 She was very ill and couldn't go to work.
11 His car is quite big and can carry eight people.
12 He put the radio on so loud that everybody in the street heard it.
13 The explanation of the meaning of the word was so difficult I couldn't understand it.
14 This small radio is powerful and can pick up stations thousands of miles away.
15 Radio reception was so poor that we didn't hear the announcement.
16 The book was so long I couldn't finish it last night.
17 His mother is quite young and may marry again.
18 The lecturer spoke so softly that people at the back of the hall couldn't hear him.

19 There were so many people in front of me that I couldn't see the procession.
20 The sun shone for quite a long time and dried up the pools of water in the streets.

4 Relatives

1 Defining and Non-defining Adjectival Clauses

In order to decide which relatives to use one should distinguish between defining and non-defining adjectival clauses.

Defining clauses tell us who or what the noun is; non-defining clauses simply give information about the noun.

Compare the following pairs of sentences:

1 (a) The professor *who described new methods of overcoming illiteracy at the Paris conference* will visit this country next month.

   (b) The Minister of Education, *who is now nearly seventy*, said he would retire soon.

2 (a) The teacher *who taught us last year* has now returned to England.

   (b) Our history teacher, *who used to live in France*, gave a talk on French politics last night.

3 (a) The book *which he borrowed last week* was a novel.

   (b) This book, *which I bought in Lagos*, has helped me with my economics.

4 (a) The furniture *which he bought last year* is already broken.

   (b) Locally made furniture, *which is much cheaper than imported furniture*, is now found in almost every home.

In the first sentence of each of the pairs the words in italics tell us precisely who or what the noun is. In the second sentence of each pair the words in italics tell us something about the noun but do not define it. Defining clauses are essential to the meaning of the sentence and if they are omitted one is inclined to ask 'Which professor?' (1(a)), 'Which teacher?' (2(a)), 'Which book?' (3(a)), and 'Which furniture?' (4(a)). On the other hand if a non-defining clause is omitted one loses only information, which, although it may be of interest, is not essential to the sentence.

(The distinction between defining and non-defining adjectival clauses is also important for punctuation. Commas are never used with defining clauses but must be used with non-defining clauses. See p. 141.)

89

2 Omission of the Relative Pronoun

Sentences 3(a) and 4(a) may be rewritten without the relative:

The book (which) he borrowed last week was a novel.

The furniture (which) he bought last year is already broken.

In these sentences the relatives were objects of verbs (*borrowed* and *bought*). In sentences 1(a) and 2(a) the relatives are subjects of verbs (*described* and *taught*). In other words the relative pronoun of a defining adjectival clause may be omitted if it is the object of a verb.

3 The Use of 'that'

Sentences 1(a), 2(a), 3(a) and 4(a) may be rewritten with *that* as the relative pronoun, although *who* is more common:

The Minister of Education *that* described new methods of overcoming illiteracy at the Paris conference will visit this country next month.

The teacher *that* taught us last year has now returned to England.

The book *that* he borrowed last week was a novel.

The furniture *that* he bought last year is already broken.

That can be used as the relative pronoun in defining adjectival clauses. In non-defining adjectival clauses we use:

who for persons (subject)

Our history teacher, *who* used to live in France, gave us a talk on French politics last night.

whom for persons (object)

Our history teacher, *whom* I saw on my way here, said he would not give us a test today.

which for things or animals

The book *which* he borrowed last week was a novel.

That is never the object of a preposition following it:

Here is the book *to which* he referred.

The joke *at which* I laughed was rather silly.

That may, however, be used if the preposition is placed at the end of the sentence or clause:

Here is the book *that* he referred *to*.

The joke *that* I laughed *at* was rather silly.

(*Note:* The construction with *that* and the preposition at the end of the defining clause is much more usual than the construction with *which* preceded by the preposition.)

4 The Possessive Relative

Use *whose* for persons, countries and towns:
> The boy *whose* pen I'm using is Usman.

Note that for things we often use a different construction – *with* instead of a relative and an adjectival clause:
> The house *with* the damaged roof is being sold.

is more normal English than:
> The house *of which* the roof is damaged is being sold.

Similarly, we may say:
> The girl *with* red hair is my sister.

5 Adverbs as Relatives

When, *where* and *why* are used in the same way as relative pronouns:
> Friday is the day *when* we have the party.
> This is the place *where* the accident happened.
> He didn't tell us the reason *why* he couldn't come.

6 'What' as a Relative

We can avoid using *the thing(s) which* and *the thing(s) that* by simply using *what*:
> He forgot *the things which* he was going to say.
> He forgot *what* he was going to say.
> *The thing that* is not clear is why he came.
> *What* is not clear is why he came.

EXERCISE 70
Complete the following sentences with suitable relatives *unless no relative is necessary* (i.e. omit the relatives wherever possible):
1 The book . . . is lying on the table is mine.
2 The water . . . he drank was dirty.
3 The letter . . . he wrote was in reply to mine.
4 Robert Mugabe, . . . became first Prime Minister of Zimbabwe, took several university degrees.
5 The car . . . I bought ten years ago is still in good working order.
6 The boy . . . was knocked down by a lorry is now in hospital.
7 Anybody . . . comes is welcome.
8 The girl . . . the Minister gave the prize to was in Form 1.
9 The girl to . . . the Minister gave the prize was in Form 1.

10 Have you completed the work ... you were given?

11 Where is the boy ... father came to see the headmaster?

12 The concert ... we attended last night was very enjoyable.

13 The hotel ... we stayed at last summer is now closed.

14 The meal ... I had last night made me ill.

15 The chair ... is standing in the corner will have to be repaired.

16 That magazine, ... is published four times a year, contains a lot of interesting articles.

17 The lecturer talked about Waugh, ... novels I have started reading.

18 Gaelic, ... is the language of the Scots, is little spoken nowadays.

19 The play, ... our English teacher is producing, will be performed five times next week.

20 The toothbrush ... he used is almost worn out.

21 This is the paragraph about ... the teacher was talking.

22 Where is the pen ... I was using this morning?

23 I haven't seen the boy ... suitcase was stolen.

24 They are painting the wall ... I usually lean my bicycle against.

25 On his way to Rome, ... he had visited before, he stopped in several Italian towns.

EXERCISE 71

Connect the following pairs of sentences, making one a relative clause but using a relative pronoun or adverb only when necessary and remembering to use essential commas:

1 This is a beautiful piece of music. It was composed by Beethoven.

2 The bomb exploded in the cinema yesterday evening. At the time there were several hundred people present.

3 The official gave me a travel warrant and some other documents. I needed them for my journey.

4 She bought a new tennis racquet. It was quite expensive.

5 Do you like this suit? I've just bought it.

6 Here are the tablets. The doctor prescribed them.

7 We crossed the river. We crossed it at a point where it was narrow.

8 He learnt to speak Amharic. It is the official language of Ethiopia.

9 He didn't give me any reason. He said I should wear a tie.

10 You were telling me about a singer. How old is he?

EXERCISE 72

1 Write five sentences requiring *which* before a non-defining adjectival clause on the model:

This pen, *which* he bought five years ago, still writes well.

2 Write five sentences requiring *who* before a non-defining adjectival clause on the model:

His best friend, *who* had known him for several years, helped him when he was in trouble.

3 Write five sentences requiring *who* before a defining adjectival clause on the model:

The girl *who* came first had worked very hard.

4 Write five sentences requiring *which* before a defining adjectival clause on the model:

The plants *which* are growing in this garden will bear fruit next year.

5 Rewrite the ten sentences in (c) and (d) substituting *that* for *who* or *which*.

6 Write five sentences using *where* as a relative before a defining or non-defining adjectival clause on the model:

The town *where* we played the final match was many kilometres away.

7 Write five sentences using *when* as a relative before a defining or non-defining adjectival clause on the model:

He remembers the day *when* the war broke out.

5 Comparatives and Superlatives

1 Sentence Patterns for Making Comparisons

There are three main ways of making comparisons:

1. Her essay is *as long as* mine.
   This book is *as interesting as the* one I read last week.
   The sentence pattern is: 'AS' + ORDINARY FORM OF THE ADJECTIVE OR ADVERB + 'AS'.

2. Her essay is *longer than* mine.
   This book is *more interesting than* the one I read last week.
   He did the exercise *more carefully than* I did.
   Sentence pattern: COMPARATIVE FORM OF THE ADJECTIVE OR ADVERB + 'THAN'.

3. Her essay is *less long than* mine.
   This book is *less interesting than* the one I read last week.
   He did the exercise *less carefully than* I did.
   Sentence pattern: 'LESS' + ORDINARY FORM OF THE ADJECTIVE OR ADVERB + 'THAN'.

Particular attention should be paid to these points:
(a) When we use the *as . . . as* pattern, the ordinary form of the adjective or adverb must be used.
(b) The comparative form of the adjective or adverb in the second pattern must be followed by *than*.
(c) The third pattern is rare. We normally express the idea of *less* by using the negative form of the first pattern:
   Her essay is *not as long as* mine.
   This book is *not as interesting as* the one I read last week.
   He *didn't* do the exercise *as carefully as* I did.
(In the negative form of this pattern we can replace the first *as* by *so*:

Her essay is *not so long as* mine.

This book is *not so interesting as* the one I read last week.

He *didn't* do the exercise *so carefully as* I did.)

Another way of avoiding the use of *less* is by using the comparative form of the adjective of opposite meaning to replace the adjective in the above sentences:

Her essay is *shorter* than mine.

This book is *duller* than the one I read last week.

He did the exercise *more carelessly* than I did.

2 Sentence Patterns with the Superlative

There are three main patterns:

1. Her essay is *the longest* of all.

    This book is *the most interesting* one I have ever read.

    He did the exercise *the most carefully* of all the boys in the class.

Sentence pattern: DEFINITE ARTICLE + SUPERLATIVE FORM OF THE ADJECTIVE OR ADVERB.

2. Her essay is *one of the longest* submitted for the competition.

    This book is *one of the most interesting* I have ever read.

Sentence pattern: 'ONE OF' + DEFINITE ARTICLE + SUPERLATIVE FORM OF ADJECTIVE.

3. Of all the essays submitted hers is *the least long*.

    Of all the books I have read this one is *the least interesting*.

    He did the exercise *the least carefully of* all the boys in the class.

Sentence pattern: DEFINITE ARTICLE + 'LEAST' + ORDINARY FORM OF ADJECTIVE OR ADVERB.

Note these points:

(a) Whereas the comparative is used to compare one or more things or persons with one other, the superlative is used to compare one or more things or persons with more than one other.

(b) *The* is nearly always used before the superlative.

(c) The superlative cannot be followed by *than*.

(d) *Most* can also mean *very*, and in this case it does not take the definite article:

    This is a most valuable coin.

    He is most helpful.

(e) *Most* sometimes has the meaning of *the majority* and in this case, too, it does not take the definite article:

    Most people I have spoken to support my suggestion.

    Most towns now have piped water.

3 Formation of the Comparative and Superlative

1. Adjectives and adverbs of one syllable (except adjectives in the form of the past participle) make the comparative and superlative by adding -er and -est:

tall	taller	tallest
big	bigger	biggest
fast	faster	fastest

but torn   more torn   most torn
here a past participle, *torn*, is used as an adjective.

2. Adjectives of two syllables ending in -y, -er and -ow and -le normally form the comparative and superlative with -er and -est:

pretty	prettier	prettiest
clever	cleverer	cleverest
narrow	narrower	narrowest
gentle	gentler	gentlest

(Note that other adjectives that follow this pattern are:
common, polite, quiet, wicked, cruel, stupid, pleasant.)

3. Adjectives of two syllables other than those ending in -y, -er, -ow and -le form the comparative and superlative with *more* and *most*:

hopeful	more hopeful	most hopeful
honest	more honest	most honest
selfish	more selfish	most selfish

4. Adjectives of three or more syllables form the comparative and superlative with *more* and *most*:

beautiful	more beautiful	most beautiful
efficient	more efficient	most efficient
attractive	more attractive	most attractive

5. Adverbs ending in -ly form the comparative and superlative with *more* and *most*:

loudly	more loudly	most loudly
rudely	more rudely	most rudely
neatly	more neatly	most neatly

(Note that *early*, when used as an adverb, forms the comparative and superlative in accordance with the rules for two-syllable adjectives and takes -er and -est.)

6. Certain adjectives and adverbs have irregular comparative and superlative forms:

good	well	better	best
bad	badly	worse	worst
much		more	most

| many | more | most |
| little | less | least |

(The forms *elder* and *eldest* are still used instead of *older* and *oldest* before brother, sister, son, daughter, grandson and granddaughter. *Elder* cannot be used before than and *older* must be used: My daughter Mary is older than my other daughter.)

EXERCISE 73
Complete the following using the *as ... as* or *so ... as* construction:
1 His writing is (untidy) mine.
2 My new watch is not (accurate) my old one.
3 This dictionary is not (useful) the one we had last year.
4 This month is (dry) it usually is.
5 She is (smart) her mother.
6 My mark was (high) yours.
7 He speaks English (well) he speaks French.
8 The bus did not leave (early) yesterday.
9 This exercise is not (difficult) I expected.
10 He does not correct his work (thoroughly) he should.

EXERCISE 74
Complete the following sentences using the *comparative adjective* or *adverb* + *than* construction:
1 He is (young) his sister.
2 Football is (exhausting) tennis.
3 The river is (shallow) it was a month ago.
4 She speaks Arabic (correctly) I do.
5 Oranges are (cheap) apples.
6 Shoes are (expensive) they were last year.
7 The school secretary types (quickly) she writes.
8 Most people understand a language (well) they speak it.
9 His health is (bad) it was last year.
10 He reads (fast) Samuel.

EXERCISE 75
Complete the following sentences using constructions with the comparative or superlative form of the adjective or adverb as necessary:
1 Lagos is (big) Kaduna.
2 America is (rich) country in the world.
3 Last term he got (high) mark in the class.
4 I find history (interesting) geography.
5 June, July and August are (wet) months in Ethiopia.
6 John stayed (long) anyone.
7 His manners are (bad) mine.

8 He has married (pretty) girl in the college.
9 John works (slowly) Olu.
10 His voice is (loud) that of any other boy in the class.
11 This is (unpleasant) medicine I have ever tasted.
12 His new typewriter is (well) made the one he sold me.
13 Usman works (hard) any boy in the class.
14 He is (selfish) person I have ever come across.
15 His father is (wealthy) man in the town.
16 My brother arrived (soon) I expected.
17 Belgium is one of (densely) populated countries in the world.
18 She found nursing (tiring) working in an office.
19 My father has (well) paid job in the company.
20 Bernard Shaw is considered (outstanding) playwright of the twentieth century.

EXERCISE 76
Complete these sentences with *as* or *than* constructions as necessary:
1 He has drunk more wine ...
2 A film is more enjoyable ...
3 A letter is not as useful ...
4 The captain of this year's football team is not as popular ...
5 The school library is better stocked ...
6 The harvest this year is not so plentiful ...
7 This year's examination will be more difficult ...
8 The climate of Sweden is as cold ...
9 The Atlantic is rougher ...
10 A jet travels faster ...
11 My new camera is more expensive ...
12 Airmail is much quicker ...
13 She spent longer on that question ...
14 He kicked the ball as hard ...
15 He turned the radio on as loud ...
16 The army advanced further ...
17 The harvest is as good this year ...
18 My grandfather lived longer ...
19 This ball-point has lasted as long ...
20 My dog barked louder ...

6 Word Order

To write and speak good English we must use not only correct grammatical forms and appropriate vocabulary but also correct word order. There are various problems presented by English word order and this section helps you revise them.

1 Adverbs

Adverbs of Place, Time and Duration

These usually come at the end of a sentence or clause:

> He met with an accident *at the crossroads*.
> While we were staying *at the hotel*, a conference was being held.
> He joined our class *last week*.
> My sister, who got married *last year*, now lives in Lagos.
> He listened to the radio *for half an hour*.
> He waited *for an hour* and then went away.

Adverbs of time and duration may be placed at the beginning of a sentence or clause, or immediately after a link word:

> *Last week* he joined our class.
> My sister, who *last year* got married, now lives in Lagos.
> *For half an hour* he listened to the radio.
> *For an hour* he waited and then went away.

Adverbs of place occasionally come at the beginning of a sentence or clause. This is especially the case with *here* and *there*:

> *Here* is the book you are looking for.
> I opened the door and *there* was my brother.

In written English other adverbs of place can come at the beginning of a sentence or clause:

Across the sand flowed a small stream.

At the bottom of the stairs lay a dead man.

Note that after an adverb of place in this position the verb is placed before the subject if the verb is intransitive and if the subject is a noun (i.e. there is normal subject-verb order if the verb is transitive or the subject of a pronoun):

Under the table a dog was eating a bone.

Here it is.

Adverbs of Frequency

Adverbs of frequency (indicating how often an event occurs) are subject to different rules. Such words are *always, often, frequently, generally, usually, occasionally, sometimes, rarely, seldom, never, ever.*

1. They are placed before the verb they modify:

He *always* works hard.

She *often* leaves without permission.

I *rarely* take a holiday.

2. They are placed after an auxiliary verb or the modals *can, could, may, might, must* and *ought*:

He has *often* forgotten his textbook.

They will *never* agree to his suggestion.

I can *sometimes* find time for reading.

The verbs *have to* and *used to* are normally preceded by the adverb:

He *often* had to borrow money.

We *always* used to light a fire in winter.

3. They are placed after the first part of the auxiliary if it consists of more than one word:

He has *often* been praised for his work.

He has *rarely* been told that he is generous.

4. They are placed after *not*:

He does not *always* work hard.

She does not *often* leave without permission.

5. They are placed after the subject in questions:

Have you *ever* been to America?

Do they *often* come to see you?

If the adverb is stressed it may be placed elsewhere in the sentence:

(a) before the auxiliary:

He *always* has done his best.

They *occasionally* have forgotten to attend.

(b) *often* can come at the end of a sentence or clause:

He visits us *often*.

I write to him *often*, but I don't get many letters from him.

(c) *never* can come at the beginning of a sentence and in this case the question order (auxiliary-subject-verb) is used:

Never have I met such a foolish person.

Never did she regret marrying him.

Certain other adverbs obey the same rules as adverbs of frequency: *almost, already, also, hardly, just, merely, nearly, not, only, quite, rather, scarcely, soon, still, therefore*.

He had *almost* finished his meal.

He has *quite* forgotten the appointment.

He is *still* trying to enter the university.

Already and *soon* can also come at the end of a sentence or clause:

We have *already* met him.

We have met him *already*.

We will *soon* reach the town.

We will reach the town *soon*.

Note that after *scarcely* or *hardly* — as with all negative adverbs at the beginning of a sentence or clause (see *never* in (c) above) — we use the question order, i.e., auxiliary-subject-verb:

Scarcely had the rain stopped when the players went out onto the field.

Hardly had the car started when something went wrong with the engine.

When the answer to the question 'how often?' is an adverbial phrase or clause giving the number of times an event occurs, the adverbial phrase or clause comes at the end of the sentence or clause (or, for emphasis, at the beginning). Examples of such phrases and clauses are:

every six months	every other day
twice a month	as often as you wish
every hour	as many times as he wants to

We have a test *every six months*.

She visits her aunt *twice a month*.

The bell rings *every hour*.

We play football *every other day*.

You may come and see us *as often as you wish*.

He may borrow my bicycle *as many times as he wants to*.

Adverbs of Manner

In a sentence with the verb in the active form an adverb of manner comes at the end:

He painted the house *very badly*.

She made the curtains *very well*.

We have packed the goods *carefully*.

If the verb is in the passive form, it is more usual to put the adverb of manner before the participle:

The house was *very badly* painted.
The curtains were *very well* made.
The goods have been *carefully* packed.

EXERCISE 77

Place the adverb in a suitable position in the sentence without emphasising it:

1 The builders have completed the house. (almost)
2 His parents arrived. (half an hour ago)
3 This student does good work. (generally)
4 I met him. (in the library)
5 He doesn't refer to a dictionary. (often)
6 He had to take the medicine. (three times a day)
7 He has heard of Marconi. (never)
8 I bought two new shirts. (in that shop)
9 He has been in hospital. (for two months)
10 Have the workmen finished painting the ceiling? (nearly)
11 Our teacher has marked these books. (just)
12 Does he go to the cinema? (every Saturday night)
13 We were able to hear what he said. (hardly)
14 She doesn't play volley ball. (still)
15 They left Ghana. (in 1981)
16 He goes to see his parents. (five times a year)
17 He can beat me at tennis. (nearly)
18 Have you glanced through the book? (merely)
19 He has explained the theory to me. (often)
20 His father got married. (twice)
21 She has attended our weekly meetings. (seldom)
22 Do you make many mistakes? (usually)
23 We will begin painting our house. (on Thursday)
24 Haven't you heard of Hemingway? (ever)
25 He has become fluent in Arabic. (already)
26 She goes to church. (as often as she can)
27 These boys may cause their teachers a lot of trouble. (sometimes)
28 The play had started when the electricity failed. (hardly)
29 I have glanced at the newspaper. (scarcely)
30 I have glanced at the newspaper. (today)
31 Has her brother been a schoolmaster? (always)
32 He has been absent. (several times this term)
33 We have a lot of work to do. (always)
34 They won't allow us our share. (ever)
35 He used to cook his own meals. (often)
36 Have you travelled by train? (ever)
37 We haven't been to Europe. (often)

38 His father had to work hard for his living. (never)
39 His father had to work hard for his living. (all his life)
40 Is he on time for appointments? (usually)
41 Has that team lost a game? (this year)
42 We would have gone to the cinema. (occasionally)
43 We have breakfast at seven. (generally)
44 Reagan became President of the U.S.A. (in 1981)
45 She gets more than half marks. (never)
46 I had given up hope of meeting him. (quite)
47 We can hear the music. (scarcely)
48 We have been practising word order. (today)
49 We have practised word order. (every day this week)
50 We have been practising word order. (just)

Order of Two Adverbs

When we wish to use an adverb of place and an adverb of time in the same sentence or clause, the usual order is *adverb of place* + *adverb of time*:

He left *for Europe last Thursday*.

She went *to the theatre last Saturday*.

If we wish to emphasise the adverb of time we may place it before the adverb of place:

He left *last Thursday for Europe*.

She went *on Saturday to the theatre*.

As mentioned above, the adverb of time can come at the beginning of the sentence or clause:

Last Thursday he left for Europe.

On Saturday she went to the theatre.

An adverb giving the number of times an event occurs normally comes before an adverb of time:

She went to the library *several times last week*.

He went fishing *every weekend last summer*.

This rule also applies when *often* is used towards the end of a sentence:

He went there *often in 1982*.

He used to come here *often last year*.

EXERCISE 78

Rearrange each of the following groups of words in the normal, unemphatic order of English sentences. The words within each pair of dashes must remain in the order they appear.

1 – to his parent's home – at weekends – often – goes – he –
2 – ploughing the field – almost – when I called on him – finished yesterday afternoon – he had –

3 – chess – this term – every Saturday – play – will – he –
4 – hardly – this year – able – be – her education – to complete – she will –
5 – the floor – nearly – have – they – in the kitchen – finished – sweeping –
(in question form)
6 – to the clinic – last month – six times – he went –
7 – thoroughly – last week – cleaned – the classrooms – were –
8 – he – in class – reminded – last year – was – to pay attention – often –
9 – to do – usually – a lot of revision – before – have – we – examinations –
10 – he was – when – at elementary school – sometimes – told he was lazy – he
was –
11 – usually – flight – from Addis Ababa – six times a week – there is –
12 – to his office – yesterday – I – went – three times –
13 – before – had – been – we – there – never –
14 – arrived – last week – on time – never – she – for her classes –
15 – worked – as he – yesterday – hard – he – a rest – is – today – at home –
taking –
16 – always – leave – six in the morning – their office – they –
17 – gets up – he – before seven o'clock – never – these days –
18 – once a week – usually – he – when he is staying in the town – at least –
visits – us –
19 – often – she – to church – twice – goes – on Sundays –
20 – finished – his speech – scarcely – had he – when – among the audience –
broke out – disorder –

2 Adjectives

Rules for the order of adjectives are less definite than those for the order of
adverbs. There are, however, a few points which can help us.

The position of the adjective depends on how closely it is related in idea to
the noun.

1. Any adjective in the form of a noun or gerund comes next to the noun it
qualifies:

    an interesting *history* book
    a cheap *transistor* radio
    some clean *drinking* water
    some new *washing* powder

Included in this class of adjective are adjectives of nationality:

    a recent *French* book
    a beautiful *Japanese* vase

2. Before adjectives in 1 above come any adjectives of colour:

a new, *red*, marking pen
a tall, *dark*, French girl

3. Next comes any adjective of size, shape or weight:
    an old, square, brown, wooden box
(In actual practice one rarely uses as many adjectives as this together.) In table
form the order is:

Other adjective	Adjective of Size, Shape or Weight	Adjective of Colour	Adjective from noun or gerund	NOUN

EXERCISE 79
Arrange the adjectives in the correct order before the noun, changing *a* to *an*
where necessary:
1 a coat (brown old)
2 a necklace (gold expensive)
3 a cow (black thin)
4 a house (new stone)
5 some oil (cooking fresh)
6 a camera (German old)
7 a road (narrow country)
8 a desk (old large)
9 a room (dirty small)
10 a lamp (gas dim)
11 a teacher (mathematics young)
12 a car (grey large American)
13 a shirt (green nylon wet)
14 an alley (dark narrow)
15 a machine (modern duplicating large)
16 a bag (empty large)
17 a watch (silver small)
18 a dress (cotton yellow cheap)
19 a jacket (leather brown untidy)
20 a carpet (beautiful multicoloured square)

7 Prepositions and Adverbial Particles

Although the best way to learn the correct use of prepositions and adverbial particles is by ample reading, listening, speaking and writing, there are certain rules which are worth knowing.

1 Prepositions of Time

'For' and 'since'

Any confusion between these two words can easily be avoided by remembering that:

> FOR is followed by a period of time
> SINCE is followed by a point of time
> He has been living in this town *for eight years.*
> He has been living in this town *since 1981.*

Both a period of time and a point of time can be expressed by a clause:

> He has been living in this town *for longer than I can remember.*
> He has been a wealthy man *since the day he inherited his father's money.*

'At', 'in' and 'on'

At is used with an exact point of time:

> The bell rang *at* ten o'clock.
> The plane touched down *at* nine fifteen.

(*At* is also used with festivals: *at* Christmas, *at* Easter, etc.)

In is used with periods of time:

> Our friends arrived *in* the evening.
> The museum will be closed *in* August.

On is used with days and with dates which include the day:

> We played football *on* Wednesday.
> The battle was fought *on* 2nd May.

In and *on* are not used before *today, yesterday, tomorrow, the day after tomorrow, last* or *next*:

We are going shopping *tomorrow*.

It rained heavily *last Monday*.

He is leaving *next Friday*.

(Notice the difference between *on time* and *in time*: *on time* means 'punctually', *in time* 'before the time appointed'.

We got to the cinema *on time*. (i.e. just before the film began)

We got to the cinema *in time* to have a talk with our friends before the film began.

In can also be used to show the period after which something will happen:

He will arrive *in* ten minutes' time.

She is leaving *in* three months' time.

'By'

When used as a preposition *by* has the meaning *not later than*:

The field must be ploughed *by* the end of this month.

It is therefore important to distinguish between *by* and *at*. Compare these two commands:

Bring the book to the office *by* ten o'clock.

Bring the book to the office *at* ten o'clock.

(Note the expression *by day* meaning *during the day*.)

EXERCISE 80

Supply *for, since, at, in, on, by* where required in the following sentences:

1 We don't do much work ... the afternoon.
2 They have lived in this village ... 1963.
3 ... his sixteenth birthday he had already passed the examination.
4 World War II broke out ... 1939.
5 The new term starts ... September 10.
6 They have lived in Nigeria ... six months.
7 It is usually much warmer ... three o'clock in the afternoon than ... the morning.
8 We went to his house ... last Thursday.
9 I have been waiting for you ... eight o'clock.
10 They got married ... June.
11 We will finish our exams ... two days' time.
12 His birthday is ... next Tuesday.
13 We have been waiting ... over half an hour.
14 ... the summer we will have our holidays.
15 They went home ... sunset.
16 I have worked hard ... the day I came to this school.
17 He drinks a lot of coffee ... the mornings.

18 . . . the anniversary of their wedding they had a party.
19 The library has been closed . . . the beginning of this week.
20 The fighting started . . . half past four . . . the morning.
21 He has to leave for America . . . the end of the month. (i.e. not later than the end of the month)
22 He left school . . . Easter.
23 His father has been ill . . . over a month.
24 His brother has been ill . . . last month.
25 The play will begin . . . half an hour.
26 The interview will take place . . . three-thirty . . . next Tuesday.
27 He has been collecting stamps . . . the age of ten.
28 Most animals eat . . . night and sleep . . . day.
29 His family have been farmers . . . four generations.
30 I plan to take the test . . . six months' time.
31 He has been living in retirement . . . several years.
32 He left the party . . . time to catch the last bus home.
33 Our bus arrived at Lagos . . . time. (i.e. punctually)
34 He went to the dentist's . . . yesterday afternoon.
35 We are going to a party . . . tomorrow evening.
36 I studied . . . two hours . . . last night.
37 I did not finish my work . . . time to check it.
38 I came here . . . six o'clock and have been waiting for you . . . then.
39 The shop will re-open . . . June.
40 She has been a teacher . . . more than five years.
41 He started his new job . . . nine o'clock . . . Monday morning.
42 He was headmaster of that school . . . fifteen years.
43 We will know the results . . . next Wednesday. (i.e. no later than next Wednesday)
44 It rained . . . three hours . . . last night.
45 She is going to get married . . . June.
46 The final match is . . . 12 June.
47 He has been ill in bed . . . six days.
48 Term ends . . . the day after tomorrow.
49 He has been studying Arabic . . . 1980.
50 The cinema was closed . . . July and August.

2 Prepositions of Place

'In' and 'at'

In suggests 'enclosed', 'within an area':
    in a box
    in the room

in London

in America

Note the expression '*in* the middle'.

At suggests 'not enclosed':

at the crossroads

at the end of the road

at the station

We often use *at* when we want to suggest that some activity is taking place:

He is working *at* his desk.

We saw a good film *at* the cinema.

The teacher is standing *at* the blackboard. (i.e. He is proposing to make use of it.)

Note that we say *in the corner of the room* but *at the corner of the road*.

EXERCISE 81

Supply *at* or *in* as required by the sense:

1 He used to live ... Lagos.

2 She lost her ring ... the sand.

3 She met her husband ... England.

4 Today there are a lot of clouds ... the sky.

5 There has been an accident ... the corner of the street.

6 He was sitting ... his desk ... the corner of the room.

7 I saw him swimming ... the lake.

8 Our house is ... the top of the hill.

9 Australia is ... the southern hemisphere.

10 There are thirty cows ... that field.

11 ... my village there are two churches.

12 I will meet you ... the signpost near my house.

13 He put his desk ... the middle of the room.

14 She was born ... a small village near Ibadan.

15 The ship was ... the Bay of Biscay when the storm broke.

16 I was ... Nairobi when the President was there.

17 A doctor happened to be ... the spot where the accident occurred.

18 There is a bus-stop ... the end of the road.

19 We were ... Kenya last month.

20 A war broke out ... Korea in 1950.

3 Exercises on Prepositions and Adverbial Particles

In Exercises 82–93 complete the sentences with the most suitable word from those listed.

1 He lent his bicycle ... a boy he hardly knew.
  A to B for C over D from E by
2 Miracles are happenings one can only wonder ...
  A on B upon C at D for E over
3 The burglar has been charged ... seven crimes.
  A from B of C by D on E with
4 He promised to pick me ... at the corner of the road on his way to town.
  A on B up C in D over E off
5 He drove from the airport to the hostel ... great speed.
  A to B by C at D in E on
6 She succeeded ... jumping the hurdle at her third attempt.
  A to B in C with D from E over
7 The librarian could not account ... the missing books.
  A about B for C up D from E of
8 Many candidates spent too much time ... the first part of the examination
  paper.
  A in B about C with D on E for
9 The common people of England had to struggle ... their rights.
  A over B against C for D on E about
10 The clerk was dismissed ... his post.
  A off B from C out D against E out of
11 Although the bell had gone we all carried ... writing.
  A with B in C on D of E on with
12 That noise is preventing me ... working.
  A from B in C by D out E of
13 He is suffering ... malaria.
  A from B of C for D with E by
14 The thief was disguised ... an official of the electricity corporation.
  A in B from C under D of E as
15 He was knocked ... as he was crossing the road.
  A into B down C to D on E off
16 After her mother died she was brought ... by her aunt.
  A into B for C up D to E through
17 While he was playing football, he had a sudden longing ... a glass of
  lemonade.
  A of B in C from D for E by
18 We are supplied ... milk every day by the farm.
  A for B with C of D by E in
19 She is jealous ... my success.
  A of B from C for D to E at
20 She was charmed ... the young man and agreed to marry him.
  A for B through C by D on E over

EXERCISE 83

1 The road was so crowded ... people that the traffic could not pass.
  A in B on C with D of E from

2 The committee arrived ... a decision after several hours' discussion.
  A into B through C to D on E at

3 Their friendship ended ... the quarrel they had last month.
  A by B at C under D with E on

4 His latest book deals ... the most difficult scientific theories.
  A about B to C over D with E by

5 He applied ... the company for a job.
  A in B from C to D into E of

6 His success started when he was introduced ... the politician.
  A over B into C from D to E at

7 The Prime Minister has left ... the conference in Paris.
  A for B to C at D on E in

8 His savings were reduced ... almost nothing by medical expenses.
  A on B to C of D over E under

9 The colonel decided to communicate ... headquarters before retreating.
  A to B on C from D onto E with

10 Have you found the solution ... the problem?
  A to B in C from D with E about

11 I didn't know that boy was related .. you.
  A on B at C by D with E to

12 The teacher was angry ... the student who came late.
  A to B with C for D from E against

13 His country was occupied ... a foreign power.
  A by B from C of D with E under

14 Our teacher did not think the book suitable ... senior students.
  A on B at C with D for E to

15 Now that he is old he is very apt ... forget.
  A by B on C from D in E to

16 He could not call himself a friend of the Minister but he was at least
  acquainted ... him.
  A with B from C on D in E to

17 He has been absent ... school for over a week.
  A of B off C out of D at E from

18 The goalkeeper was ashamed ... letting the ball through.
  A on B of C to D by E from

19 He wrote his answer ... ink.
  A with B in C on D of E by

20 She was disqualified ... the examination because she cheated.
  A for B from C by D against E out

1 She played ... the school team last season.

A by   B from   C at   D in   E under

2 The prisoners escaped ... jail last night.

A over   B out   C from   D into   E out of

3 The boy who got full marks was suspected ... cheating.

A with   B by   C for   D about   E of

4 The teacher pointed ... the student's tense mistakes.

A into   B over   C on   D out   E off

5 The manager insisted ... knowing what the clerk had been doing all morning.

A in   B on   C by   D from   E to

6 He is longing ... the day when he will be able to earn his own living.

A by   B to   C for   D on   E out

7 He was excluded ... the examination because he had forgotten his identity card.

A out   B out of   C from   D into   E on

8 He recovered ... his illness only last week.

A over   B from   C up   D against   E on

9 He prefers volley ball ... football.

A from   B over   C against   D upon   E to

10 The doctor dissuaded him ... travelling.

A against   B from   C in   D into   E for

11 The prisoner was accused ... murder.

A with   B of   C on   D for   E from

12 The judge decided to deprive the convict ... his rights as a citizen.

A to   B off   C from   D of   E with

13 The preacher tried to attract attention ... speaking in a loud voice.

A in   B by   C through   D from   E with

14 The Director hinted ... the possibility of a holiday next week.

A at   B to   C of   D over   E up

15 He has cared ... his old father since 1979.

A over   B for   C of   D to   E after

16 The doctor advised him to abstain ... alcohol.

A from   B to   C on   D off   E in

17 The teacher was disappointed ... the work of the class.

A for   B with   C on   D about   E through

18 She was considered well qualified ... the post.

A for   B to   C by   D from   E on

19 He said that he was grateful ... all the help we had given him.

A with   B of   C from   D for   E by

20 Where he lives now is remote ... the city.

A on   B in   C for   D of   E from

EXERCISE 85

1 The habit of getting up late grew ... her.
  A on B to C through D onto E in

2 My younger brother seems to delight ... making a noise when I am studying.
  A over B in C on D from E with

3 My father was very annoyed ... me.
  A from B of C with D at E against

4 He was quite content ... the mark he got in the test.
  A for B about C on D in E with

5 The headmaster congratulated him on the way he had carried ... his duties as a prefect.
  A out B with C through D about E over

6 He apologised ... not keeping the appointment.
  A in B about C on D for E from

7 The teacher praised him ... his hard work.
  A with B of C on D over E for

8 I reminded him ... his promise.
  A of B from C with D by E over

9 The prisoner tried to conceal the truth ... the judge.
  A on B by C from D of E behind

10 He changed ... a suit before going to the party.
  A to B into C by D with E on

11 The wall protected our soldiers ... the enemy bullets.
  A with B from C on D by E off

12 After trying hard several times, he met ... success.
  A with B up C upon D in E about

13 The knife was hidden ... the small boy.
  A against B to C from D at E away

14 He married a girl he had been friendly ... for some years.
  A to B for C of D from E with

15 Our school has increased ... size during the last few years.
  A in B by C to D on E up

16 This boy is unable to distinguish a verb ... a noun.
  A with B against C from D to E by

17 He had a quarrel ... his brother.
  A against B by C from D with E to

18 His fear ... dogs was quite ridiculous.
  A about B from C of D by E to

19 She is capable ... cooking quite a good meal.
  A in B for C from D on E of

20 He now lives quite close ... the mosque.
  A on B about C at D to E from

1 He expressed his liking ... modern novels.
  A to B with C for D through E on
2 At eight o'clock the men were hard ... work.
  A in B of C with D by E at
3 There is a danger that his illness will develop ... something more serious.
  A into B to C for D through E on
4 That young man is eager ... promotion.
  A for B to C with D over E of
5 He was loyal ... his country.
  A for B to C of D from E by
6 The man bowed ... the chief.
  A about B over C to D at E upon
7 His efforts resulted ... success.
  A to B in C for D on E with
8 He is not familiar ... the works of Shakespeare.
  A on B in C about D with E by
9 Small nations have often been the victims ... oppression.
  A from B for C of D by E through
10 The teacher responsible ... the school magazine takes us for English.
  A to B from C for D about E with
11 That criminal was convicted ... a crime when he was seventeen.
  A by B with C for D on E of
12 I don't know what has become ... John since he left school.
  A from B to C on D about E of
13 Since their quarrel they no longer speak ... one another.
  A among B with C to D at E by
14 The team decided to withdraw ... the league.
  A from B to C out D out of E off
15 The trader was extravagant and ran ... debt.
  A for B about C over D into E after
16 He was warned ... the danger but he ignored it.
  A of B from C on D upon E at
17 I asked him his opinion ... the new book of poems.
  A on B over C in D of E to
18 That he was at the cinema on the night of the crime is proof ... his innocence.
  A of B about C from D to E against
19 He has been interested ... stamp-collecting for many years.
  A on B in C at D to E about
20 The subject was ... discussion when I arrived.
  A in B on C under D at E before

1 He said he had been offended . . . the speaker.
   A at B by C about D with E from
2 That professor is famous . . . his book on India.
   A for B over C about D from E with
3 I am very concerned . . . my unemployed brother.
   A from B of C about D to E at
4 The soldier was punished . . . neglect of duty.
   A from B of C over D for E by
5 His father did not approve . . . his conduct.
   A to B on C by D from E of
6 Telephone her and tell her she has left her glasses . . .
   A about B behind C over D up E on
7 Although the men were armed . . . the latest weapons, they were defeated.
   A by B of C from D with E on
8 He dived . . . the lake to save his brother who was drowning.
   A to B upon C through D into E over
9 A tree in our garden was struck . . . lightning.
   A from B of C on D by E with
10 His father was converted . . . Christianity when he was still a boy.
   A into B to C by D about E on
11 While he was standing at the bus-stop he was unable to shelter . . . the rain.
   A in B from C over D against E out of
12 The boy was saved . . . the sharks by a tourist.
   A against B from C by D over E off
13 Before he went to his house, we were told to beware . . . the dog.
   A about B on C from D off E of
14 The President did not refer . . . the coming election in his speech.
   A to B about C on D at E into
15 The plane touched . . . at six o'clock.
   A on B under C down D off E in
16 He has not yet replied . . . the letter we sent him last week.
   A for B at C on D to E over
17 The policeman restrained the two boys . . . fighting.
   A from B for C on D in E about
18 His teacher criticised him . . . carelessness.
   A about B for C on D of E with
19 She made a good impression . . . her teachers last year.
   A by B to C into D on E over
20 The workers had been agitating . . . better conditions since 1980.
   A at B for C over D by E to

EXERCISE 88

1 He persisted ... his folly despite all the advice I gave him.
  A to   B in   C about   D at   E from

2 The new teacher is very popular ... his students.
  A into   B from   C with   D by   E over

3 After the examination he disposed ... his textbooks.
  A with   B for   C out   D of   E from

4 He was amazed ... what had happened.
  A from   B at   C for   D with   E of

5 That boy bores me because he is always boasting ... his achievements.
  A of   B off   C from   D on   E by

6 The teacher made no comment ... the boy's work.
  A to   B on   C against   D from   E over

7 He complained ... pains in his stomach.
  A for   B about   C through   D of   E from

8 He complained ... the noise his neighbours were making.
  A on   B over   C with   D about   E from

9 He glories ... his past successes.
  A about   B of   C in   D on   E for

10 He trusted his servant ... a large sum of money.
  A with   B to   C of   D through   E for

11 We mistook him ... the gardener.
  A with   B of   C on   D for   E as

12 He will have to answer ... his actions.
  A for   B of   C to   D about   E on

13 A friend is a person you should be able to count ... when you are in difficulties.
  A by   B in   C for   D with   E on

14 The doctor operated ... the injured man.
  A on   B in   C for   D to   E into

15 I marvel ... the amount of work he has done.
  A to   B for   C of   D with   E at

16 The manager deduced ... what he was told that the clerk was dishonest.
  A by   B from   C to   D on   E with

17 I am indebted ... him for the help he gave me when I was ill.
  A with   B to   C of   D under   E in

18 He asked a question that was not relevant ... what we were discussing.
  A on   B in   C for   D to   E about

19 I have little confidence ... his ability.
  A for   B to   C in   D about   E of

20 ... the last occasion we had a meeting only a few people came.
  A by   B at   C in   D over   E on

116

1 He never joins ... our games.

   A with B in C of D off E up

2 The President conferred ... the Prime Minister on the crisis.

   A to B of C from D by E with

3 I concluded ... what I heard that he would be late.

   A on B in C from D with E by

4 I do not always agree ... him.

   A to B with C on D of E from

5 I furnished the police ... all the information I had.

   A with B to C of D from E by

6 When she was twenty-one her father yielded ... her wishes and allowed her to marry.

   A against B from C at D to E about

7 She despaired ... ever becoming a nurse.

   A to B out C with D of E from

8 I was very impressed ... his ability to work hard.

   A with B for C on D in E about

9 The headmaster said that he did not expect a boy to lean ... a wall when speaking to him.

   A by B at C onto D to E against

10 It was very kind ... you to help me.

   A by B of C for D to E about

11 He was quite overcome ... sorrow when he heard the news of his brother's death.

   A at B of C for D against E with

12 He was very envious ... his cousin.

   A from B to C of D over E against

13 I am very obliged ... him for helping me to get that job.

   A for B from C with D by E to

14 The President was accompanied ... several army officers.

   A from B of C by D with E for

15 It is a pity that book doesn't contain a key ... the exercises.

   A on B from C with D to E about

16 My new house is built ... brick.

   A by B in C of D from E to

17 This year there has been a decrease ... the number of books sold.

   A over B in C for D from E by

18 The headmaster said he disapproved ... boys wearing slippers in school.

   A for B from C to D of E against

19 The lawyer warned him that by making such a statement he would be guilty ... an offence against the law.

   A of B from C with D to E on

20 He is very slow ... arithmetic.

    A of B for C at D with E on

EXERCISE 90

1 He is too absorbed ... his work to have time for hobbies.

    A through B about C of D from E in

2 He has established a reputation ... hard work.

    A in B on C for D of E about

3 The facts were laid ... the judge.

    A to B before C on D for E at

4 We are convinced ... the need for an investigation.

    A for B from C of D by E on

5 Not all the boys attended ... the lesson.

    A to B for C of D on E from

6 H. G. Wells was a contemporary ... Bernard Shaw.

    A for B on C in D of E by

7 Animals are not completely devoid ... intelligence.

    A in B on C with D of E for

8 It was thoughtful ... him to invite us.

    A for B from C of D with E by

9 The teacher was always patient .. boys who tried hard.

    A on B for C of D from E with

10 Our French master has translated 'Macbeth' ... French.

    A out of B to C into D for E on

11 He has been corresponding ... a boy in England for over a year.

    A to B at C for D from E with

12 When I asked him if he liked Arab music, he said that he was quite indifferent ... it.

    A on B at C to D from E by

13 His parents no longer have much influence ... him.

    A about B over C to D at E from

14 I have considerable doubts ... his honesty.

    A on B in C for D about E to

15 The clerk was blamed ... the untidy state of the files.

    A about B for C of D on E against

16 He gave me three Italian stamps ... exchange for a rare Russian one.

    A with B by C for D in E on

17 He was in the habit of going ... a stroll every evening.

    A in B by C to D on E for

18 Several members of the expedition to the South Pole perished ... the cold.

    A with B by C from D of E under

19 He likes to show ... his knowledge of languages.

    A with B about C of D off E up

20 The headmaster entrusted the mathematics master ... the task of preparing the new timetable.

A with B on C in D for E from

 1 New students must enrol ... the course next Wednesday.
   A for B in C on D into E to
 2 Over one thousand people perished ... the earthquake.
   A through B at C in D by E with
 3 He decided ... legal action to protect his own reputation.
   A about B on C with D at E for
 4 My brother has now retired and lives ... a small pension.
   A from B on C by D with E for
 5 He argued that he was quite innocent ... the charge.
   A from B about C with D to E of
 6 He had a lot of experience ... teaching before he came to this school.
   A from B of C by D for E at
 7 She is very good ... mathematics.
   A in B to C for D at E with
 8 He merely glanced ... the chapter before the test.
   A into B on C up D at E by
 9 We were shocked when we saw our bill amounted ... such a large sum.
   A about B to C up D up to E into
10 The petrol tank burst ... flames when a cigarette end fell into it.
   A out B into C to D in E out of
11 The traveller was robbed ... all his money.
   A out B on C from D of E by
12 The mechanic said he would see ... my car.
   A for B to C on D with E up
13 He was delighted ... the result of the examination.
   A for B on C from D with E in
14 He joked ... his chances of passing the examination.
   A of B for C to D about E with
15 The prince succeeded ... the throne.
   A for B on C to D by E into
16 He was anxious ... his father's health.
   A to B of C with D on E about
17 She was intent ... passing the examination.
   A to B from C for D on E by
18 In his speech the Prime Minister only touched ... the new taxes.
   A about B in C for D on E into
19 He hopes to proceed ... his studies when he recovers from his illness.
   A at B with C to D for E on

20 He hopes to proceed ... the university later this year.
   A on   B at   C through   D with   E to

EXERCISE 92

1 The police are enquiring ... the case.
   A into   B in   C over   D for   E on

2 Living in the desert, he found his food deficient ... vitamins.
   A on   B in   C for   D of   E from

3 My cousin seemed to be very annoyed ... my remark.
   A by   B from   C on   D through   E against

4 You shouldn't judge him ... his behaviour last night.
   A in   B with   C over   D by   E from

5 I have forgotten her name but I know her ... sight.
   A from   B by   C in   D for   E at

6 The captain congratulated him ... his performance.
   A about   B in   C over   D on   E by

7 He benefited ... the holiday he spent with his son.
   A in   B on   C over   D by   E from

8 The teacher demanded an explanation ... the student.
   A from   B for   C on   D to   E against

9 She has been troubled ... her health for some months now.
   A from   B about   C against   D by   E for

10 She said she was very glad ... the help we had given her.
   A of   B by   C at   D from   E on

11 Now that he has a family to support, he is not as well ... as he used to be.
   A on   B off   C in   D up   E with

12 He has a real genius ... mathematics.
   A in   B at   C for   D on   E from

13 There was nothing he could do ... the circumstances.
   A by   B at   C for   D on   E in

14 The speaker expressed his gratitude ... the reception he had been given.
   A to   B with   C for   D by   E about

15 There is no known treatment ... that disease.
   A against   B from   C to   D by   E for

16 There are so many exceptions ... that rule that I wonder if it is worth knowing.
   A from   B by   C in   D for   E to

17 He invested all his money ... one company.
   A at   B on   C into   D in   E to

18 He was charged ... theft.
   A for   B with   C of   D from   E on

19 I can't see to read ... the light of this candle.
   A in   B by   C from   D on   E through

20 Our car collided ... a lorry on the way here.

   A against B at C on D into E with

 1 You should show some consideration ... the feelings of others.

   A about B for C to D on E from

 2 He has cultivated a taste ... good music.

   A for B in C at D from E of

 3 He is quite alarmed ... recent political events.

   A at B from C of D for E on

 4 His likeness ... his brother is quite remarkable.

   A on B by C for D to E with

 5 I assured him ... my intention to join the club.

   A for B on C about D to E of

 6 Students who do well in this examination will be exempt ... the final in December.

   A of B to C for D from E with

 7 His father is ill ... malaria.

   A of B from C with D over E in

 8 I would have been very hard ... if I had not found a job.

   A over B up C off D at E about

 9 The police could not find any witnesses ... the accident.

   A by B to C about D on E of

10 The thief was sentenced ... five years' imprisonment.

   A on B for C by D in E to

11 The soldiers were ... the mercy of the enemy.

   A at B under C by D on E with

12 A friend will stand ... you in times of trouble.

   A on B for C by D up E against

13 The policeman was told to watch ... a tall man with one arm.

   A from B on C about D out for E off

14 The patient was confined ... bed for a week.

   A in B from C to D into E off

15 She failed ... her attempt to swim the river.

   A from B in C on D with E out

16 The police rounded ... the thieves.

   A over B away C off D up E in

17 He was relieved ... the good news.

   A through B for C at D over E from

18 The government imposed a new tax ... luxuries.

   A on B of C in D over E for

19 My brother is working ... a thesis for an advanced degree.

   A in B on C out D onto E for

20 The Pope often appears ... public.

    A at   B by   C for   D in   E on

EXERCISE 94

Substitute for the verb *in italics* the same tense of *go* with one of the following:

    down   out of   on   out   about

    off   up   on with   with   back on

Example: He *descended* the stairs to the cellar.

             He went down the stairs to the cellar.

1 The liner *sank* two days after leaving port.

2 He *failed to keep* his promise.

3 As time *passed*, he became well known in local politics.

4 The bomb *exploded* as the guests were leaving.

5 We *continued* our lesson after the interruption.

6 The fire *did not cease burning* until three in the morning.

7 The headmaster *left* his office an hour ago.

8 He *accompanied* me to Europe.

9 The preacher *travelled from place to place* telling the people to repent.

10 The cost of living *increased* last year.

EXERCISE 95

Substitute for the verb *in italics* the same tense of *make* with one of the following:

    off   with   up   for   out   off with

1 I cannot *understand* this message, which is written in code.

2 Some boys *stole* our clothes while we were swimming.

3 The two girls *ended* their quarrel and became good friends once again.

4 He *went towards* the door.

5 Could you *understand* what he was saying?

EXERCISE 96

Substitute for the verb *in italics* the same tense of *give* with one of the following:

    out   up   in   away   back

1 The teacher *resigned* his job when he fell ill.

2 He said he would not *yield* to our demands.

3 He *revealed* the secret to the police.

4 The teacher *distributed* the new books yesterday morning.

5 I *returned* the book last week.

EXERCISE 97

Substitute for the verb *in italics* the same tense of *turn* with one of the following:

    over   away   down   out   upside down

1 He arrived late and *was refused admission*.
2 The small boat *capsized* in the storm.
3 He was *rejected* by the committee.
4 Coming into the office, he found everything *disarranged*.
5 The suggestion *proved* to be a good one.

EXERCISE 98
Substitute for the verb *in italics* the same tense of *take* with one of the following:
      over   after   off   to   up
1 Nobody can say that he *resembles* his father.
2 He *grew to like* his job after some months.
3 His brother *began* swimming when he was sixteen.
4 The new manager *assumed control of* the business last month.
5 The plane *began its flight* at seven this morning.

EXERCISE 99
Substitute for the verb *in italics* the same tense of *look* with one of the following:
      after   into   for   up to   upon
1 The police *are investigating* the criminal's past.
2 They *admired* their captain.
3 He *provided for* his parents.
4 We all *considered* him a lazy person.
5 We *searched for* his pen.

EXERCISE 100
Substitute for the verb *in italics* the same tense of *come* with one of the following:
      to   into   out   across   up to
1 A brilliant idea *entered* his head while he was shaving
2 The next issue of the magazine *appears* early next month.
3 I *found* an interesting book in the library the other day.
4 A man who was obviously a tourist *approached* me and asked me the way to the market.
5 His bill *amounted to* more than he could afford.

EXERCISE 101
Substitute for the verb *in italics* the same tense of *let* with one of the following:
      off   in   down   out
1 Nobody will be *admitted* after the play has begun.
2 Thousands of fireworks *were exploded* during the festival.
3 She *failed* her parents when she refused to help them financially despite all her promises.

4 Although he was obviously guilty, the young prisoner *was discharged without being punished*.

5 The Minister *revealed* the details of the tax changes.

EXERCISE 102

Substitute for the verb *in italics* the same tense of *break* with one of the following:

     down   out   in   off   up

1 World War II *began* in 1939.

2 The crowd *dispersed* when the rain began to fall.

3 She *collapsed* when she heard the sad news.

4 Thieves *entered* and stole ten typewriters.

5 The Government decided *to end* diplomatic relations with France.

EXERCISE 103

In each of the gaps in the following sentences supply the most suitable word from this list:

     out   up   out for   upon   off

1 The doctor was set ... by a dog as he entered the patient's house.

2 His work is always neatly set ...

3 A boy set a firework ... in the classroom.

4 The traders at the market set ... their stalls.

5 Before he set ... the town, it began to rain.

EXERCISE 104

In each of the gaps in the following sentences supply the most suitable word from this list:

     on   through   over   up   away

1 She got ... her illness.

2 His father asked him how he was getting ... at school.

3 All the boarders have to get ... at six o'clock.

4 A convict got ... last week.

5 The headmaster told the boy he would have to get ... an entrance examination.

EXERCISE 105

In each of the gaps in the following sentences supply the most suitable word from this list:

     in   up   out   up with   off

1 The nightwatchman tried to put ... the fire.

2 Our headmaster does not put ... bad behaviour.

3 We wrote to say we could not put him ... and he would have to stay in a hotel.

4 He put ... his application yesterday.

5 The match was put ... for a week because of bad weather.

EXERCISE 106

In each of the gaps in the following sentences supply the most suitable word from this list:

    up   down   out   over   away with

1 The drinks ran ... before the party was over.
2 While she was staying at the hotel, she ran ... an enormous bill.
3 The treasurer of the club ran ... the funds.
4 The doctor told the man he was run ... because of overwork.
5 The water in the sink ran ... and the kitchen was flooded.

8 Spelling

In the writer's experience about a third of the mistakes made by the average student in written work in his final year at secondary school are spelling mistakes. Even when the main difficulties of grammar and syntax have been mastered, spelling mistakes continue to spoil every piece of written work to such an extent that some students despair of ever becoming reasonably good spellers.

There is much that one can do to improve one's spelling in a fairly short time. There are certain general rules that are well worth learning. In addition, there are some three hundred common words which are frequently misspelt but not covered by any rule; if these words are studied and practised, there is soon a considerable improvement in one's spelling. A list of these words can also be used for reference purposes.

(You will already be aware that there are some differences between British and American spelling. This is not important; in fact, only about three per cent of words are affected. The chief differences are the double -*l*- of British spelling, shown as an exception to Rule 3, -*or* in place of -*our* of British spelling (as in color, colour), and final -*er* in place of -*re* of British spelling (as in center, centre). Both forms are correct, but you should try to be consistent.)

1 Rules of Spelling

(*Note*: A *prefix* is a group of letters placed at the beginning of a word, a *suffix* a group of letters placed at the end of a word.)

1. A word ending with a silent *e* loses the *e* if a suffix beginning with a vowel is added:

hate	hating
like	liking

write   writer
continue   continuation

If the suffix begins with a consonant, the *e* is not dropped, e.g. *extremely*, *encouragement*.

Exceptions: We can spell judgement with or without an *e*.

           Argument drops the *e*.

           The *e* is retained after *c* or *g* to keep the consonant 'soft', e.g. *changeable, noticeable*.

2. The suffix *-ful* has only one *l*:

delightful   playful
beautiful   hopeful

3. If we add a suffix beginning with a vowel to a single consonant, we double the final consonant providing the preceding syllable is stressed and contains a single vowel.

be*gin*   beginning
pre*fer*   preferred
o*mit*   omitted
for*bid*   forbidden

Obviously, if the word has only one syllable, contains a single vowel and ends with a single consonant, this rule must apply:

sit   sitting
big   bigger

When the final syllable is unstressed we do not double the final consonant:

*dif*fer   differed
*mer*it   merited
*cred*it   credited

When the final syllable has two vowels or ends with two consonants, we do not double the final consonant:

toil   toiled
select   selected

Exceptions: (i) A final *l* after a single vowel is doubled even if the preceding syllable is not stressed, e.g. *travel, travelled*. This applies only in British spelling, not in American.

          (ii) A final *p* is doubled in kidnap, handicap and worship even though the stress falls on the first syllable in these words.

4. When *-ly* is added to an adjective ending in *-l* to form an adverb, the result is a double *l*, e.g. *delightfully, successfully, orally*.

5. When a prefix ends with the same letter as the first letter of the word it is placed before, the result is doubling:

mis- misspelt   *un-* unnoticed
il- illegal   *im-* immeasurable

6. When the suffix *-ness* is added to a word ending in *-n*, the result is a double *n*, e.g. *keenness*, *meanness*.

7. *I* before *e*
   Except after *c*
but only when *ie* or *ei* are pronounced like *ee* in bee:
   deceive   believe
   receive   relieve
Exceptions: Seize, counterfeit, weird.

8. A certain group of verbs contain *s* while their corresponding nouns contain *c*:
   verbs   *nouns*
   advise   advice
   prophesy   prophecy

9. Final *ie* is changed to *y* when *-ing* is added:
   lie   lying
   die   dying

10. When a suffix is added to a word of more than one syllable ending in *-y*, the *y* changes to *i*:
    happy   happiness
    study   studious
-y is retained before a suffix beginning with *i*, e.g. *studying*.

11. When a word ends in a 'hard' *-c* (i.e. pronounced like the *c* in cat) we add a *k* before the suffix beginning with *e*, *i* or *y*:
    picnic   picnicking
    panic   panicking

12. *Q* is always followed by *u*, e.g. *quantity*, *equation*.

13. There are only three verbs ending in *-ceed*. These are *succeed*, *exceed*, *proceed*.
All other verbs with the final syllable pronounced in this way end with *-cede*, e.g. *concede*, *precede*, *recede*.

14. A final *-y* preceded by a consonant is changed to *-ies* in the plural:
    cry   cries   country   countries
If the *y* is preceded by a vowel, it remains *y* in the plural:
    donkey   donkeys   monkey   monkeys

15. Certain irregular plurals should be noted:
    analysis   analyses
    basis   bases
    crisis   crises
    oasis   oases

stimulus	stimuli
hippopotamus	hippopotami

Words ending in *-o* are a source of difficulty. Some form their plurals by simply adding *-s*:

piano	pianos
solo	solos
dynamo	dynamos
photo	photos
radio	radios
kilo	kilos

Others take the plural ending *-oes*:

cargo	cargoes
echo	echoes
hero	heroes
mosquito	mosquitoes
motto	mottoes
potato	potatoes
tomato	tomatoes
volcano	volcanoes

16. Special care is required with words which are sometimes one composite word and at other times two separate words:

every body and *everybody*.

Every body is adjective + noun; used in this way, *body* means *corpse* or *group of persons or things*. The form *everybody* is a pronoun, meaning *all the people*:

Every body was washed before burial.

Everybody who took the examination passed.

every one and *everyone*

Every one means *each one*; everyone means *all of them*:

Every one of the six boys went swimming.

Everyone who left late missed the bus.

every day and *everyday*

Every day is an adjective + noun; everyday is an adjective, meaning *happening daily*.

Every day this week has been hot.

A visit by an angry customer is an everyday event in that shop.

all together and *altogether*

All together means *everybody or everything at the same time or in company*; altogether is an adverb meaning *entirely, on the whole*:

All together there were seven hundred people present.

His poem is altogether too difficult for me to understand.

all ready and *already*

All ready means *completely ready*; already is an adverb with the meaning *before now (or then)*, *as early as now (or then)*:

The bus is all ready to leave.

I have already spoken to the manager.

all right

All right means satisfactory, or, in common speech, O.K. The form *alright* is increasingly used.

in fact, *in order*

must each be written as two separate words.

in spite of, *in front of*

must each be written as three separate words.

2 Words Frequently Misspelt

abbreviate
absence
academic
accelerate
accept
accommodate
accompany
accomplish
accurate
accuracy
acquaintance
acquire
acquit
across
address
administration
advantage
aeroplane
alcohol
allege
analyse
angel
   (religion)
angle
   (maths.)
ankle
annually

anonymous
anxiety
anxious
apologise
appal
apparatus
appearance
appetite
appreciate
appropriate
arduous
arithmetic
artificial
athlete
athletics
artifical
audience
available
awkward

bachelor
baggage
balance
balloon
banana
bargain
behaviour

benefit
bicycle
boundary
boycott
bruise
burglar
bury
business

canoe
captain
career
carpentry
catastrophe
category
ceiling
cement
cemetery
ceremony
certificate
challenge
channel
character
cleanliness
cocoa
colleague
college

collision
colloquial
column
commemorate
commercial
committee
compel
compete
competitor
completion
comprehension
compulsory
conference
connection
conscience
conscientious
conscious
continuous
convenient
correspondence
correspondent
cough
create
curiosity
curious

deceased
  (dead)
definite
delegate
delicious
democracy
dependent
describe
description
desert
desperate
destroy
destruction
deteriorate
develop
development
dialogue

dictionary
disaster
disastrous
disappear
disappoint
discipline
diseased
  (sick)
dispel
distinguish
distribution
dormitory
duly

earnest
economics
economy
efficient
eighth
elementary
eligible
embarrass
eminent
enemy
engineer
entrance
exaggerate
excel
excellent
except
exercise
existence
expel
expense
experience
experiment
explanation

familiar
fascinate
favourite
fiery
financial

forehead
foreign
foresight
forty
fourteen
friend
fuel
fundamental

gallop
goal
government
governor
grammar
gramophone
grateful
grief
guarantee

happiness
harass
height
holiday
humour
humorous
hundred
hygiene
hygienic

ignorance
illegal
illegible
illiterate
immediately
independence
independent
indispensable
infinite
infinity
influential
innocence
innocent
inoculate

integrity
intelligence
interpret
interrupt
item

jail
jealousy

knowledge

laboratory
laborious
laundry
leisure
library
librarian
lightning
likelihood
literally
literature
livelihood
loathe
loneliness
loyalty
luggage

magnificent
maintenance
malaria
marriage
marvellous
massacre
mathematics
medicine
messenger
miniature
ministry
mischief
mischievous
missionary
modern
monotonous

monstrous
months
moreover
moustache
muscle
museum
mysterious

necessary
necessity
neglect
neighbour
ninety
ninth
nuisance

occasion
omission
opinion
opponent
opportunity
opposite
oppressor
original
orphan

paid
parallel
paralyse
parasite
parliament
participate
passenger
pastime
patriotic
persuade
physical
pigeon
pleasure
possess
possession
presence
privilege

procedure
proceedings
process
profession
professor
pronounce
pronunciation
propagate
psychology
punctual
pursue

quarrel
queer
quiet
quite
quotation

recommend
religious
remedy
remembrance
repetition
representative
resistance
responsible
restaurant
rhyme
rhythm

salary
sandal
scarcely
scarcity
scene
scenery
scissors
secondary
secretary
separate
similar
simultaneous
slaughter

solemn
sparsity
speak (vb.)
speech (n.)
statement
strenuous
strict
stubborn
subtle
success
sufficient
summary
supplement
surprise
surrender
surround
suspicious
syllable
sympathise
sympathy
systematic

technical

technician
technique
temperature
temporary
tenant
therefore
thorough
till
tolerate
tough
traffic
traveller
tremendous
truly
tuition
twelfth

unanimous
unique
until

vacation
(holiday)

vaccinate
valuable
variety
various
vegetable
vegetation
vehicle
vigorous
visible
vocation
(calling)
voluntary
volunteer

welcome
welfare
withhold
witness
wooden
wool
woollen
wreck

Homophones

Some words are pronounced alike but spelt differently:
assistance (*aid*)   assistants (*helpers*)
bare (*naked*)   bear (*carry, animal*)
boarder (*person living in a place*)   border (*edge*)
bow (*bend*)   bough (*of tree*)
brake (*of vehicle*)   break (*smash*)
cite (*mention*)   sight (*sense of seeing, what is seen*)   site (*place*)
complement (*what completes*)   compliment (*polite word*)
council (*group*)   counsel (*advice*)
course (*direction, of study*)   coarse (*rough*)
currant (*fruit*)   current (*flow*)
die (*opposite of live*)   dye (*to make material a certain colour*)
heal (*cure*)   heel (*of foot*)
hear (*with ears*)   here (*this place*)
pair (*two of the same kind*)   pear (*the fruit*)
peace (*opposite of war*)   piece (*bit*)
plain (*level land, clear, ordinary*)   plane (*aeroplane, level*)
principal (*chief*)   principle (*basic truth, rule, law*)

sew (*with cotton*)   sow (*seeds*)
stationary (*motionless*)   stationery (*paper and envelopes*)
straight (*not bent*)   strait (*narrow water passage*)
there (*in that place*)   their (*of them*)   they're (*they are*)
waist (*of the body*)   waste (*not use profitably*)
weak (*opposite of strong*)   week (*seven days*)
wear (*use as clothing*)   where (*in what place*)
weather (*natural conditions*)   whether (*if*)
weight (*heaviness*)   wait (*defer action*)

EXERCISE 107
In each of the following sentences one word is misspelt. Give the correct
spelling and state the relevant rule.
1 He did his work very carefuly.
2 The lawyer informed him that what he suggested was ilegal.
3 Our house is biger than theirs.
4 He showed more keeness than I expected.
5 The Principal told all the boys to go to the dinning-room.
6 Immediately he entered the room the boys stood up.
7 There was only a handfull of people present.
8 I do not beleive a word he says.
9 The teacher adviced the students to correct their work.
10 There is no doubt that the prisoner was lieing when he made the
statement.
11 He was considered to be the lazyest boy in the class.
12 The heros returned from the war.
13 He shiverred as he stood waiting for the bus.
14 His mistakes are not very noticable.
15 He has been writeing a composition since four o'clock.
16 I recieved his letter last Monday.
17 There are many mosquitos in the area where he lives.
18 He did a lot of unecessary work.
19 He refered to the dictionary only once while reading that poem.
20 All the students were successfull in the examination.
21 The speaker qoted Bernard Shaw.
22 They entertainned their friends last night.
23 He spent all his money at the begining of the term.
24 Candidates will be informed officially of the result in April.
25 He felt greatly releived when he received the letter.
26 His absence went unoticed.
27 He succeded where others had failed.
28 His sister had reached marriagable age.
29 Some of the candidates had forgoten to bring their pens.

30 The room smelt stuffy as many people had been smokeing.
31 I did extremly well last term.
32 No student is permited to use the library after nine o'clock.
33 We sailled our boat a hundred miles down the river.
34 There are now four radioes in our school.
35 The Industryal Revolution first took place in England.
36 The scientist invented a useful devise.
37 The old man's relations were with him when he lay dieing.
38 He sufferred a great deal at the hands of the enemy.
39 Inspite of trying hard he was unsuccessful.
40 The candidate concceded defeat.

EXERCISE 108
Which is required in the gaps in the following sentences – *every day* or
everyday?
1 It is an ... occurrence.
2 It happens ....
3 I go there ....
4 For a soldier hardship may be an ... experience.
5 Soldiers may suffer hardship ....

EXERCISE 109
Which is required in the gaps in the following sentences — *all together* or
altogether?
1 This is an ... insoluble problem.
2 ... no less than two thousand students entered the competition.
3 His brother is ... too mean.
4 The weather changed ... last week.
5 He put his exercise books ... in a box.

EXERCISE 110
Which is required in the gaps in the following sentences – *all ready* or *already*?
1 Are the letters ... for posting?
2 The players are ... to begin.
3 The books are ... for distribution.
4 It has ... rained.
5 He had ... been told.

EXERCISE 111
Which is required in the gaps in the following sentences – *every body* or
everybody?
1 The headmaster said that ... should leave the school by five o'clock.
2 ... in the mortuary is washed before burial.
3 ... who works in a mortuary soon becomes accustomed to seeing dead
  bodies.

4 The biology master told the boys to write notes on ... they had dissected that term.
5 ... I have met agrees with me on the subject.

EXERCISE 112
Which is required in the gaps in the following sentences – *every one* or *everyone*?
1 Has ... arrived?
2 ... of those boys has been in this school over four years.
3 ... I met at the party was enjoying himself.
4 During the journey ... of the bottles was broken.
5 The referee said the match could not continue until ... of the players was ready.

EXERCISE 113
Study these sentences in preparation for dictation:
  1 In spite of what he maintained I was quite sure everybody thought a burglary was an everyday occurrence.
  2 Beginning his essay late at night in order not to be interrupted, he felt so tired that his handwriting was almost illegible.
  3 The speaker argued that his opponent had exaggerated the achievements of the former government.
  4 His use of colloquial English is sometimes quite humorous.
  5 The procedure to be followed on such occasions has already been described by a member of the committee.
  6 Although he had in fact worked conscientiously, the examination proved a catastrophe.
  7 Separate accommodation is a privilege delegates should not expect.
  8 A person who preferred to remain anonymous paid for the expense of the conference.
  9 Every body which was lying on the ground was buried.
  10 Lightning struck in front of the professor's temporary residence.
  11 The journey across the desert proved disastrous.
  12 I was disappointed to hear that he had not had the foresight to get inoculated.
  13 Two vehicles were in collision on the road which runs parallel to the one where we live.
  14 The economic development of the country was paralysed by widespread strikes.
  15 We harassed the enemy until they had to surrender.
  16 The speech of the representative of Ghana was simultaneously translated into three languages.
  17 The loyalty of the speaker to the principles of democracy was questioned by a member of parliament.

18 He has distinguished himself by his excellent work.

19 A few months ago he bought a gramophone and some language records in order to improve his pronunciation of English.

20 As soon as our messenger returned from the laundry we gave him a pair of scissors to cut the string of the parcel.

21 A mischievous boy has upset our apparatus in the laboratory.

22 Our school librarian always has a lot of correspondence from the Ministry of Education to answer.

23 The missionary now has two assistants, both of whom have a good knowledge of medicine.

24 The principal complimented him on his achievement.

25 He left his luggage at the entrance to the dormitory.

26 The athletes competed for a prize offered by a commercial organisation.

27 He was fascinated by literature and devoted all his leisure hours to it.

28 He lost both his livelihood and his possessions in the disaster.

29 The traveller found it necessary to have his baggage sent ahead.

30 The secretary benefited from the course in mathematics.

9 Punctuation

Once you have mastered the basic rules, punctuation is largely a matter of being careful. You are more likely to be careful if you realise how important punctuation is. It is not mere decoration, and it can, in fact, change the meaning of a group of words. How many ways can you punctuate the following (without changing the order of the words or adding or omitting any words)?

Mary said I travelled by bus.

In the following sections the main difficulties of punctuation are revised.

1 The Full Stop

This is used at the end of a sentence. It is, of course, necessary to know what a sentence is in order to apply this rule. The barest minimum of grammatical knowledge is needed. A sentence is a group of words containing a subject and a finite verb, which make complete sense when they stand alone. (A finite verb is simply a verb in the form of one of the tenses and is therefore easily recognised.) Consider the following:

I want to become a teacher/because I like children.

In this sentence there are two verbs in the form of the tenses – *want* and *like* – and both have the subject *I*. *I want to become a teacher* could stand alone and form a complete sentence. On the other hand, *because I like children* could not stand alone. If a person said simply *because I like children* one would want to ask him to explain what he meant. These words are only part of a sentence. A common mistake is to write:

I wrote to Usman, he is studying in America.

Here the words after the commas can stand alone and they form a complete sentence. There should therefore be a full stop after Usman:

I wrote to Usman. He is studying in America.

Alternatively, instead of *he*, the relative *who* could be used:

I wrote to Usman, who is studying in America.

Who is studying in America cannot stand alone (unless it is a question).

Such mistakes in the use of the full stop may appear very obvious when one's attention is drawn to them, but they are mistakes that are often made.

The full stop is also used in abbreviations:

H.E. His Excellency   U.S.A. United States of America

M A. Master of Arts   i.e. id est (Latin – that is)

After abbreviations which begin with the first and end with the last letter of the word the full stop is optional:

Mr   Mrs   Dr   *or*   Mr.   Mrs.   Dr.

EXERCISE 114

Supply full stops or change commas to full stops or full stops to commas where necessary:

1 The M.P. visited this town last week, he often used to come here, but recently he has been too busy.

2 William Rogers Ph D, a noted authority on nineteenth-century literature, will lecture here next week, if he speaks as well as he usually does, we will have an interesting evening.

3 Most of the students are boys, some are over eighteen.

4 Some people live to eat. While others eat to live.

5 H E the German Ambassador, who has spent five years in this country, has been transferred to Peru, he visited that country in 1979.

2 The Question Mark

This is used only after *direct* questions (i.e. questions that are not reported):

Have you been to America?

Have they won the match?

Indirect or reported questions do not take a question mark:

He asked me if I had been to America.

I wonder if they have won the match.

3 The Exclamation Mark

This is used after words which are shouted and after expressions of surprise·

Come here at once!

What a clever boy you are!

Add question marks or exclamation marks where necessary:
1 He wanted to know if I had seen the headmaster.
2 How very foolish of you to think that he would arrive on time.
3 I heard the commands shouted in the barracks: "Attention. Quick march. Stand at ease."
4 "Did you hear the chairman say, 'The fee will be raised next year'."
5 If only I had known before today.

4 Capital Letters

These are used:
(a) *at the beginning of a sentence.* If we use direct speech after a reporting section, we must begin the spoken sentence with another capital letter:
> He opened the door and called out, "Is there anybody here?"
(b) *for all proper nouns and proper adjectives:*
> France   French
and for abbreviations of proper nouns and adjectives:
> B.B.C.
(c) *for all titles applied to one particular person:*
> Our President met the Egyptian President.
> I hear Professor Smith is leaving.
(d) *for all words in titles of books, plays, poems, etc.*, except unimportant words like prepositions, articles, conjunctions, unless one of these words is the first word:
> A History of the Sudan in the Nineteenth Century

5 The Comma

This is used:
(a) *in lists.* The lists can be of nouns, adjectives, clauses, etc:
> He plays football, tennis, volley-ball and hockey.
> A tall, thin, ugly man entered the room.
> He came into the library, walked to the history section, searched for a book, saw it wasn't there and left.

(A comma may also be placed before *and* in the above sentences but this is optional.)
(b) *after participial phrases* (either past or present)
> Chained to a post, the dog was unable to attack the thieves.
> Looking through his collection of stamps, he discovered that some had been stolen.

(c) *between two main clauses* connected by *and, but, or, nor* if the clauses are fairly long:

> He lived in Russia for several years before the war, but he learnt only a few words of the language.

(d) *after an adverbial clause* if a main clause follows:

> Although he had worked for the company for several years, he did not get promotion.

If the adverbial clause comes after the main clause, a comma is not necessary:

> He did not get promotion although he had worked for the company for several years.

(e) before and after an adjectival clause which does not define the noun but simply gives us information about it:

> His father, *who used to live in the country*, has now joined him in the town.
>
> Our Minister of Health, *who returned from New York last week*, has spent most of the last month abroad.
>
> The book *which I borrowed last month* was about coins.
>
> The Minister of Health *who came to this country in January* signed an agreement for the supply of doctors.

In the first two sentences the adjectival clauses (in italics) simply tell us more about the noun and do not answer questions like 'Who?' 'Which?'. The other two sentences contain adjectival clauses which tell us which book and which Minister of Health is referred to.

(f) before and after words in apposition to a noun (i.e. words which come after the noun and explain or describe it):

> Ernest Hemingway, *a leading American novelist*, died in 1961.
>
> My new typewriter, *an Olivetti*, is working very well.

If the words in apposition form a clause (i.e. have a subject and a finite verb) commas are not used:

> The suggestion *that the next meeting should take place on Friday* was rejected.

(g) *with words which are added to a sentence by way of comment* and are not essential to the structure:

> A few of us, *by the way*, will be unable to come.
>
> All of them, *I believe*, would agree with us.

Commonly used in this way are words like moreover, however, indeed, incidentally.

(h) *after 'yes' and 'no'*:

> *Yes*, he does smoke a lot.
>
> *No*, they never go to that cinema.

(i) *with words used to address a person*:

> *Usman*, can you hear me?

> I forgot to remind you, *John*, that we are going to the cinema tonight.

(j) *to separate the items of a date:*

> Saturday, 14 May, 1983

(The comma after May is omitted by many writers and may be considered optional.)

(k) *in addresses* (see pp. 153–4 of Chapter 10)

(l) *with direct speech:*

> "We shall leave early," he said.
>
> He said, "We shall leave early."

If the spoken sentence is interrupted for the reporting verb, another comma is required:

> "We shall leave early," he said, "as we don't want to miss the bus."

But if the speech continues with a new sentence, a full stop is used in place of this extra comma:

> "We shall leave early," he said. "We don't want to miss the bus."

EXERCISE 116

Insert commas and use capital letters where necessary in the following:

1 have you written your composition yet john?
2 haile selassie i emperor of ethiopia visited ghana in 1965.
3 my brother has visited london bristol manchester oxford and cambridge.
4 although he worked very hard for the examination he did not pass.
5 "I do not believe you john" said the teacher "when you say that this is your own work."
6 having been expelled from school he found it very difficult to get a job.
7 his mother who used to work as a nurse looked after him well when he was sick.
8 mr d.g. ogendo m.a.
  p.o. box 20916
  nairobi
  kenya
9 "moreover ladies and gentlemen" the politician declared "we must look at our government's record in foreign affairs and compare it with that of the previous government."
10 mrs thatcher the prime minister of great britain had long discussions with the prime minister of zimbabwe who was on a visit to europe.
11 looking through the telescope the student saw the planet mars.
12 having been warned about his work on three previous occasions the clerk was not surprised when he was given notice.
13 the essay which I wrote last night was for our new english teacher mr rogers but the one I am writing now is for the school magazine.
14 the proposal that games should be voluntary was made by a senior prefect.
15 all the pictures in our school exhibition are of course by the students.

16 however hard he tries no first-year student will ever be able to understand such a difficult book.

17 the servant swept the floor dusted the bookshelves cooked the meal and laid the table.

18 he said that he would always be willing to help boys who helped themselves.

19 joining the school late in the year stephen found it very difficult to retain his place.

20 while mr edeli the headmaster was addressing the whole school he suddenly fainted.

6 The Semi-colon

This is used between two closely connected main clauses:

There was not a cloud in the sky; it was extremely hot.

It would not be incorrect to use a full stop instead of the semi-colon in this example. The writer uses the semi-colon for the sake of style.

Certain words like *nevertheless, therefore, so, moreover, furthermore, thus, consequently, besides* are often used to show a close connection between two clauses and are preceded by a semi-colon and followed by a comma:

The question papers had been lost; consequently, the examination could not take place.

7 The Colon

This is used:

(a) *to introduce a quotation:*

Bernard Shaw said: "Those who can, do, and those who can't, teach."

(b) *to introduce words which explain what has already been referred to:*

She now had several choices open to her: she could enter a teachers' training college, take a secretarial course, or continue her studies with a view to getting a degree.

The words which come after the colon explain what *the several choices* were. Used in this way the colon frequently introduces a list:

He told me the subjects he had taken for the examination: English, history, geography, general science and mathematics.

8 Quotation Marks

These are used:

(a) *before and after words of direct speech:*

"Don't forget to bring your own pens with you," our teacher said.

Note that if a reporting verb interrupts the direct speech the quotation marks must be closed before the reporting words and then reopened:

"Don't forget to bring your own pens," the teacher said, "since only writing paper will be provided."

Note also that all punctuation of the sentence of speech comes inside the quotation marks whereas punctuation not belonging to the speech comes outside them. Compare:

The headmaster said, "There will be a film show this evening."

Did you hear the headmaster say, "There will be a film show this evening"?

(b) *to indicate that the words enclosed by the quotation marks are a quotation:*

Politicians should never forget that 'a week is a long time in politics'.

(c) *for titles of books, plays, poems, articles, etc.:*

'Oliver Twist'   'Hamlet'   'Ode to a Nightingale'

In typed material it is customary to underline titles; in printed material italics would be used.

(d) *for words not accepted as normal English*, especially words from other languages used because there is no English equivalent:

Yorubas wear 'agbadas'; Sudanese wear 'gellabias'.

Again in typing we would underline, and in print use italics.

There is no fixed rule telling when to use double and single quotation marks. We should, however, be consistent. If double quotation marks are used for speech, single should be used for quotation, titles and words not accepted as normal English.

EXERCISE 117

Supply quotation marks, commas, question marks, full stops and captital letters and paragraph where required:

1 The teacher told the boys to stand up when I come into the room
2 The teacher told the boys to stand up when he came into the room
3 Come early I said so that we can have a meal together before we go out
4 Come early I said if you do we'll be able to have a meal together before we go out
5 You should refer to your dictionary our teacher told us whenever you are not sure of the spelling of a word use it also to look up words you don't know the meaning of if those words prevent you from understanding what a whole passage is about

6 Have you read my article in the school magazine usman asked his brother not yet I only got the magazine a few minutes ago do please read it as soon as you can you will see that I have referred to you in it

7 Have you read things fall apart adam asked his father no I don't get much time for reading these days

8 Which way africa the lecturer began was the title of a book published some years ago

9 I took the baccalaureat when I was sixteen the french boy told us this is the school leaving examination in france he went on to explain and a very difficult examination it is

10 Is it true that the headmaster said he wouldn't let us have a holiday next friday mary asked me

9 The Apostrophe

This is used:

(a) *to show omission of one or more letters:*

> hasn't isn't can't

Note that there is both a gap and an apostrophe.

(b) *to show possession:*

> Mohammed's book

Note the position of the apostrophe in the plural:

boys' games	ladies' clothes
children's games	men's clothes

(c) *for the plural of letters and figures:*

> r's How many r's are there in referred?
>
> 1930's I can't remember the exact date but it happened in the 1930's.

(N.B. *It's* is the shortened form of *it is*; *its* is possessive – of it; *its'* only exists as a mistake.)

10 The Dash

This is used:

(a) if in making up a sentence the speaker or writer decides *to interrupt the normal grammatical structure* to add something:

> The doctor — and I agree with him — has ordered my father to take a month's rest.

(b) *To show that a sentence was not completed* (usually because it was interrupted by another speaker):

> Somebody in the audience said, ''I should like to ask if —''

"I am sorry," interrupted the chairman, "but our time is up and no further questions can be allowed."

11 The Hyphen

This is used:
(a) *in composite words* (i.e. words made up of more than one word):
    living-room   twenty-one
    brother-in-law   ninety-six
    full-length
    life-size
(b) *when a word is begun on one line and fin-ished on the next*, e.g. 'finished' in this sentence.

It is wise to avoid this practice unless you are quite sure what the component parts of a word are. By starting a word on a new line you avoid making the mistake of splitting up a word in the wrong way. Alternatively, a dictionary will be of help.

General Exercises on Punctuation

EXERCISE 118
Punctuate and paragraph the following passages. All speech has been printed in italics to help you.
1. when the district commissioner arrived at okonkwo's compound at the head of an armed band of soldiers and court messengers he found a small crowd of men he commanded them to come outside and they obeyed without a murmur *which among you is called okonkwo* he asked through his interpreter *he is not here* replied obierika *where is he he is not here* obierika shouted the commissioner became angry and red in the face he warned the men that unless they produced okonkwo forthwith he would lock them all up the men murmured among themselves and obierika spoke again *we can take you where he is and perhaps your men will help us* the commissioner did not understand what obierika meant when he said *perhaps your men can help us* one of the most infuriating habits of these people was their love of superfluous words he thought

From *Things Fall Apart* by Chinua Achebe

2. as soon as adam was inside the courtyard he saw his father sheikh ahmed in a chair on the verandah as he approached the old man lifted his head and gazed at him dully *ive been waiting for you* he said adam stood over him his brief-case in his hand at the ministry of education they had told him that he was to leave for another town in ten days time and that a seat had already been booked for him on the plane looking down on the old man he could not tell

him the news sheikh ahmed made an impatient gesture and said irritably *we can go inside and talk* he reached for his stick and ignoring his sons offer of support lifted himself out of the chair *your uncle yousif was here* sheikh ahmed announced as he lowered himself into another chair adam inquired after the health of his uncle and each member of the family *they are well and your cousin omer has written a letter* sheikh ahmed handed his son the letter while his son was reading it he mentioned that nafisa had been asked for in marriage

From *Jangara* by John Sawkins

3. his mother called him she was a small black woman with a bold but grave face one could tell by her small eyes full of life and warmth that she had once been beautiful *would you like to go to school o mother* he gasped half fearing that the woman might withdraw her words there was a little silence till she said *we are poor you know that yes mother* his heart pounded against his ribs slightly his voice was shaky *so you wont be getting a mid-day meal like other children I understand* he said *you wont bring shame to me by one day refusing to attend school o mother ill never bring shame to you just let me get there I like school* he said this quietly his mother understood him *all right youll begin on monday as soon as your father gets his pay well go to the shops and ill buy you a shirt and a pair of shorts*

From *Weep Not, Child* by James Ngugi

4. the agent began to question me as though I were before a grand jury *whats your full name* he asked *reul john mugo gatheru* I replied *how did you come to the united states by way of india and england* I answered *why didnt you come to the united states directly from kenya instead of going to india* he asked *after I was offered a scholarship at roosevelt college I went to the american consul in nairobi to seek for information about the u s student visa the american consul advised me that in order to obtain a student visa I had to get a certificate of good conduct or political clearance from the kenya government I tried to obtain the necessary clearance but all in vain hence I went to India with the hope that if I did not obtain a u s visa I could further my higher education in india who financed your trip to india* he asked *my friends and relatives* I replied the interrogation lasted from 11 15 a m until 2 p m the man was friendly I took his cigarettes and I smoked them but I was very angry at some of his questions in fact I was very angry about the whole procedure I asked him what was behind all this and he said it was just a routine matter and that I should not worry this was hardly the truth as I discovered later.

From *Child of Two Worlds* by Mugo Gatheru

EXERCISE 119

In each of the following groups only one of the five alternatives is correctly punctuated. Which is it?

1 A I told him that, he was wrong.
   B I told him, that he was wrong.
   C I told him that, "He was wrong."
   D I told him that he was wrong.
   E I told him, "That he was wrong."

2 A He has typed the letter? hasn't he
   B He has typed the letter, hasn't he?
   C He has typed the letter, has'nt he?
   D He has typed the letter hasn't he?
   E He has typed the letter? hasn't he?

3 A "Have you seen him?" Asked John.
   B "Have you seen him"? asked John.
   C "Have you seen him" Asked John.
   D "Have you seen him," asked John?
   E "Have you seen him?" asked John.

4 A Ahmed collects stamps, he has over a thousand.
   B Ahmed collects stamps. He has over a thousand.
   C Ahmed collects stamps; He has over a thousand.
   D Ahmed collects stamps: He has over a thousand.
   E Ahmed collects stamps he has over a thousand.

5 A Children's books are often read by old ladies'.
   B Children's books are often read by old lady's.
   C Childrens' books are often read by old ladies.
   D Children's books are often read by old ladies.
   E Children's books are often read by old ladys.

6 A I don't believe a word, you say.
   B I do'nt believe a word you say.
   C I dont believe a word you say.
   D I don't believe a word you say.
   E I dont believe a word, you say.

7 A "Have you read 'Macbeth' "?
   B "Have you read 'Macbeth?' "
   C "Have you read 'Macbeth'?"
   D "Have you read 'Macbeth' "
   E "Have you read? 'Macbeth' "

8 A He asked where the dining-room was.
   B He asked where the dining-room was?
   C He asked, where the dining-room was.
   D He asked, where the dining-room was?
   E He asked, "Where the dining-room was?"

9 A He cann't swim at all.
  B He can't swim at all.
  C He cann't swim, at all.
  D He cant swim at all.
  E He can't swim, at all.

10 A Its' a pity we have only a months holiday.
   B It's a pity we have only a months holiday.
   C Its a pity we have only a month's holiday.
   D It's a pity we have only a month's holiday.
   E It's a pity we have only a months' holiday.

11 A Which desks are ours? he asked.
   B "Which desks are ours'?" he asked.
   C Which desks are ours' he asked.
   D "Which desks are ours?" he asked.
   E "Which desks are our's?" he asked.

12 A Digging in the garden, he found a five hundred year old coin.
   B Digging in the garden, he found a five-hundred year-old coin.
   C Digging in the garden, he found a five hundred-year-old coin.
   D Digging in the garden, he found a five-hundred-year-old coin.
   E Digging in the garden, he found a five hundred year-old coin.

13 A What he has just said does not convince me.
   B What he has just said, does not convince me.
   C What he has just said! Does not convince me.
   D What he has just said, does not convince me!
   E What he has just said: does not convince me.

14 A However good he is at tennis he won't be able to beat me I'm quite sure.
   B However, good he is at tennis, he won't be able to beat me, I'm quite sure.
   C However, good he is at tennis, he won't be able to beat me I'm quite sure.
   D However good he is at tennis, he won't be able to beat me, I'm quite sure.
   E However, good he is at tennis he won't be able to beat me, I'm quite sure.

15 A "What an interesting book this is!" Exclaimed Peter.
   B "What an interesting book this is" exclaimed Peter.
   C "What an interesting book this is!" exclaimed Peter.
   D "What an interesting book this is"! Exclaimed Peter.
   E "What an interesting book this is"! exclaimed Peter.

16 A He plays several games; volley-ball, tennis, football and cricket.
  B He plays several games: volley-ball, tennis, football and cricket.
  C He plays several games, volley-ball, tennis, football and cricket.
  D He plays several games. Volley-ball, tennis, football and cricket.
  E He plays several games volley-ball, tennis, football and cricket.

17 A Do you know how to spell preferred?
  B Do you know how to spell 'preferred?'
  C 'Do you know how to spell preferred'?
  D 'Do you know how to spell preferred?'
  E Do you know how to spell 'preferred'?

18 A "We have been in the cinema over twenty minutes now," said John,
    "And the film hasn't started yet."
  B "We have been in the cinema over twenty minutes now," said John,
    "and the film hasn't started yet."
  C "We have been in the cinema over twenty minutes now," Said John,
    "and the film hasn't started yet."
  D "We have been in the cinema over twenty minutes now," said John.
    "and the film hasn't started yet."
  E "We have been in the cinema over twenty minutes now, said John, and
    the film hasn't started yet."

19 A David Wilson President of the Literary Society will give a Lecture
    tomorrow evening.
  B David Wilson, President of the Literary Society, will give a lecture
    tomorrow evening.
  C David Wilson, president of the Literary Society, will give a lecture
    tomorrow evening.
  D David Wilson president of the Literary Society will give a lecture
    tomorrow evening.
  E David Wilson, president of the literary society, will give a lecture
    tomorrow evening.

20 A He told me that, Mr. Atkins, who is our new English teacher, used to
    live in Norway.
  B He told me that, Mr. Atkins who is our new English teacher used to live
    in Norway.
  C He told me that Mr. Atkins who is our new English teacher used to live
    in Norway.
  D He told me that Mr. Atkins, who is our new English teacher, used to live
    in Norway.
  E He told me that, "Mr. Atkins, who is our new English teacher, used to
    live in Norway.

21 A We shouldn't, however, agree with everything he says.
   B We shouldn't however, agree with everything he says.
   C We shouldn't, however agree with everything he says.
   D We should'nt, however agree with everything he says.
   E We should'nt however, agree with everything he says.

22 A "Where are the letters, which you wanted me to post?" Mary asked her father.
   B "Where are the letters which you wanted me to post?" Mary asked her father.
   C "Where are the letters, which you wanted me to post?," Mary asked her father.
   D "Where are the letters which you wanted me to post?," Mary asked her father.
   E "Where are the letters which you wanted me to post? Mary asked her father.

23 A "Open your books at page ten," the teacher began, "do exercises six and seven."
   B "Open your books at page ten," the teacher began. "Do exercises six and seven."
   C "Open your books at page ten," the teacher began, "Do exercises six and seven."
   D "Open your books at page ten, the teacher began, do exercises six and seven."
   E "Open your books at page ten," the teacher began; "do exercises six and seven."

24 A I think he worked as hard as I did; nevertheless, he failed.
   B I think, he worked as hard as I did, nevertheless, he failed.
   C I think he worked as hard as I did nevertheless he failed.
   D I think he worked as hard as I did, nevertheless he failed.
   E I think he worked as hard as I did. Nevertheless he failed.

25 A "How foolish of me to forget my Passport!" he exclaimed.
   B "How foolish of me to forget my passport!" he exclaimed.
   C "How foolish of me to forget my Passport," he exclaimed!
   D "How foolish of me to forget my passport," he exclaimed!
   E "How foolish of me to forget my passport" he exclaimed.

10 Letter Writing

No matter what occupation you take up after you leave school you will find that you have to write letters. People rarely write compositions once their formal education is finished, but they go on writing letters all their lives. It is therefore most important that you write good letters.

1 Personal Letters

Letter are of two main kinds: personal and business. For both kinds there are certain customs that should be observed — the address, the date, the greeting, the conclusion.

Let us look at a typical personal letter:

P.O. Box 1357,
Abeokuta,
Nigeria.
15th August 1982

Dear John,

Many thanks for your letter. I was very glad to hear that you had done so well in your exams. Let me send you my hearty congratulations. You certainly deserved this result as I know you worked very hard.

You ask how I have been spending the time since I took my exams. I have been waiting so eagerly for the results that, I must admit, I have not done half the things I planned to do during this extended holiday. Why do examiners take so long to make up their minds?

However, I have been doing a lot of reading. There were so many different things I was interested in when I was at school and did not have the time to read about because they were not on the syllabus. I have read two books about geology, which is a fascinating subject. I hope to make a hobby of geology when I get to the university. It will make a change from the study of law. I have also read several novels, mostly modern ones by authors like Graham Greene, C. S. Forester and Somerset Maugham. How enjoyable it is to read a book for pleasure and not for an examination! I have not given a thought to law, and not read one book about the subject. I shall have four long years at the university to devote to it.

I have also been going once or twice a week to the National Boys' Club. I took part in the table-tennis tournament, but I did not do very well, I'm afraid. I have been playing football for the Club every Sunday afternoon.

I will certainly let you know my exam results as soon as I have them. But don't wait for me to write before you write. I must say that I become less confident about the results each day. It was encouraging to hear that this was the case with you, and since you did so well perhaps there is still hope for me!

Yours sincerely,
Taiwo

Points in Personal Letters

There are certain points to note about this personal letter:

The writer's address should go in the top right-hand corner and there may be a comma at the end of each line (except the last, which has a full stop). The commas are by no means necessary and you may omit them if you wish. Some people prefer to begin each line of the address at the same distance from the edge of the paper:

P.O. Box 1357,
Abeokuta,
Nigeria.

You may use either this method or the one used in Taiwo's letter. Note that it is wrong to put one's own name with the address. The name of the country is included in the address only when the letter is being sent abroad.

The date should be written slightly to the left or immediately under the address after leaving a gap of one or two lines. Alternative methods of writing the date are:

15.8.82   15/8/82   August 15 1982   15th August 1982   August 15th 1982

The salutation is put at the beginning of a line after a gap of one or two lines and followed by a comma. For people we know well we can use the form *My dear John*. For close relations *My dearest Mohammed* can be used.

The main body of the letter will, of course, depend on the person it is being sent to. Remember that letter-writing is similar to conversation, and we should adopt the style we should use if we were talking to the person we are writing to. The style of this letter is friendly. There is no attempt to impress by the use of long words or flowery expressions. Nor are there unnecessary expressions like

'I am glad to write you this letter', 'I hope you are well, as I am' and 'Well, I will close now'. Personal letters are generally intended for the exchange of ideas (again, like conversation). Note that Taiwo refers to John's letter frequently and answers his questions. He arranged his ideas in paragraphs so that they will be read easily.

The ending of the letter is written in the middle of the page a line or two below the last line of the main body of the letter. *Yours sincerely* can be used for most personal letters. *Yours* is also common. *Yours ever* can be used when writing to a person you have known a long time. For a close relation one can use *Yours affectionately*.

The signature consists simply of the writer's first name since John would call Taiwo by his first name in conversation. In signing one's name there is no virtue in being illegible. Writing one's name with a great flourish or scrawl is merely a sign of vanity.

Note that in a personal letter we do not include the address of the person to whom the letter is being sent.

The Envelope

Taiwo would address his envelope in this way:

Mr. John Attafuah,
P.O. Box 298,
Cape Coast,
GHANA.

The commas at the end of each line could be omitted, and each line of the address could start at the same distance from the edge of the envelope. The person's title (Mr., Mrs., Miss, Ms., Master, Dr., Rev., etc.) should be placed before the name. The age at which Master should cease to be used for a boy is a matter of opinion, but most boys prefer to be called Mr. as early as possible. In some countries Esq. is used for gentlemen, and this is placed after the name; since it is an abbreviation of Esquire it can be followed by a full stop.

It is advisable to put your own name and address on the envelope so that it can be returned to you by the postal authorities if it does not reach its destination. Probably the best place for this is at the back of the envelope in one line at the top.:

From: Taiwo Lasebikan, P.O. Box 1357, Abeokuta, Nigeria

Note that when referring to oneself it is not customary to use a title. Women sometimes put either Mrs., Miss or Ms. in brackets after their name.

Useful Phrases for Personal Letters

When writing personal letters you may find the following phrases useful:

Many thanks for you letter

I'm very sorry not to have written before

I apologise for the delay in writing

It was good to hear from you again

I was glad to hear that . . .

I put off writing to you until . . .

I should be grateful if you would

It was very kind of you to go to the trouble of . . .

I look forward to hearing from you . . .

Just a few lines to let you know . . .

Our letters must have crossed in the post

My last letter must have got lost in the post

I had intended writing before this but . . .

Give my regards to . . .

Remember me to . . .

With best wishes

With all good wishes

EXERCISE 120

Write a letter to an uncle who has promised to help you financially when you continue your studies beyond their present level. Tell him of your plans for the next three or four years and state what you expect your financial needs will be. Your uncle is only willing to help you if you do exceptionally well in your studies. Describe the attempts you have made to obtain a scholarship or grant.

EXERCISE 121

Write a letter to a pen-friend who is coming to visit your country for two weeks. He has told you the time he will arrive at your nearest airport or railway station. He has not met you before but has seen photographs of you. Tell him what you will be wearing when you go to meet him so that he will recognise you. In case he misses you, describe how he could travel from the airport or railway station to your home.

EXERCISE 122

Write a letter to a former teacher of yours who left the school two years ago and has written to ask you how you spent these two years. Tell him (or her) about the progress you have made in your studies, the part you have taken in sports and other activities, and the changes in the school.

EXERCISE 123

Write a letter to a friend of yours at present on a short visit to England, asking him to bring back a book which you have been unable to obtain locally.

Write a reply to the following letter addressed to yourself:

28 Richmond Road,
Redhill,
Surrey,
England.
10 March 19__

Dear

You will perhaps be surprised to receive a letter from an English boy you have never heard of. While your English teacher was on a visit to England he came to my school, and I had the opportunity of speaking to him after he had watched one of our lessons. I told him that I was very interested in your country, and he therefore suggested that I should write to you.

First, let me tell you something about myself. I am sixteen years of age and in Form V of Redhill Comprehensive School. Like you, I take the Certificate examination this year. I hope to stay on at school and enter Form VI. Later I plan to go to the University of London to study medicine. My father is a doctor.

I should be very interested to hear about your country, especially about your schools. Your teacher told me that they are not unlike our schools. He said that a few of the teachers in your country are from England. Are most of the schools in your country government or private? We have both private schools and schools run by local government authorities; most children go to the latter. What games do you play? What clubs exist for after-school activities?

I do hope we will become pen-friends at least. Perhaps one day we will have an opportunity of meeting.

Give my best wishes to your English teacher.

Yours sincerely,
John Rogers

2 Business Letters

Let us now look at a business letter:

P.O. Box 891,
Nairobi.
27 September 1982

The Manager,
United Bank of Africa
P.O. Box 98,
Nairobi.

Dear Sir,

I have seen your advertisement in 'The East African Standard' for a clerk in your branch of the United Bank of Africa, and I should like to submit an application.

I am eighteen years of age and a Form V student at St. Finbarr's College, Nairobi. I am taking the School Certificate examination this November in seven subjects including Mathematics and English. I have been a prefect for over a year, and I am captain of the school First Eleven in football.

The following gentlemen have kindly agreed to send you confidential references: Mr. David Mboya, Headmaster of St. Finbarr's College; Mr. Joseph Ochwada, Senior Master of Mathematics at St. Finbarr's College; and Rev. Fr. D. J. Slattery, who has known me personally for eight years.

Yours faithfully,
Francis Mbiyu

Points on Business Letters

Note the following:

The writer's address and the date. The remarks made for the personal letter apply here.

The name and address of the person to receive the letter should appear on the left-hand side of the paper next to the margin one or two lines lower than the date; alternatively it can be written on the left-hand side of the paper next to the margin at the end of the letter. The commas at the end of each line are optional. The reason for including the name or position and address of the person to receive the letter is that a business letter can be considered a legal document and there should be no doubt about whom it is intended for. The letter may be taken out of its envelope by the clerk, and if there is no indication on the letter itself of the person it is addressed to, there may be confusion.

The salutation. Unless we have met the Manager and he is well known to us, we should begin the letter *Dear Sir* or, rather more formally, *Sir*. If we are writing a business letter addressed to a company and not an individual, we use *Dear Sirs* or, using American style, *Gentlemen*.

The main body of the letter does not contain formal and meaningless English. In a business letter, as indeed in all letters, we should aim to write clear and simple English. Naturally one's style is not conversational, but this does not mean that it should be artificial and stilted.

Do not use expressions like	Use instead
I beg to inform you	I wish to inform you
Your communication	Your letter
re	regarding
Yours of 21st inst.	Your letter of 21st
	September (*current month*)
Your obedient servant	Yours faithfully

Expressions such as those in the first column were common in the nineteenth century and have been retained by unfashionable people in the twentieth. By using them you give much the same impression you would give if you now wore nineteenth-century English clothes.

The ending of the letter. The standard form is *Yours faithfully*. *Yours truly* can also be used.

The signature should, of course, be neat and legible. What you write depends on the customs of your own country; in most cases this will be your first name followed by your surname or family name. Some people prefer to write the initial letter(s) of their first name(s).

EXERCISE 125
Answer three of these advertisements:

ARMY OFFICERS. The Ministry of Defence invites applications from secondary-school leavers who wish to train as army officers. Only students with outstanding school careers should apply. Special importance will be attached to leadership qualities and a record of achievement in sport. Apply Ministry of Defence.

CLERKS. Intelligent and industrious boys or girls required as clerks. Must have (or obtain this year) School Certificates with credits in English and Maths. Will be required to learn shorthand and typing. Good promotion prospects. Apply Anglomex Co.

CLERKS. Temporary work during the long vacation. A few vacancies exist for temporary clerks in the Ministry of Education. Students awaiting results of School Certificate may apply.

ENGINEERS. School-leavers are invited to apply for posts as trainee engineers with the Posts, Telephones and Telegraph Department. Candidates must have (or obtain this year) School Certificate with credits in Maths and Science. Good promotion prospects.

LIBRARIAN. A school librarian is required. Applicants must have (or obtain this year) a good School Certificate with credit in English. Experience as a library prefect would be a recommendation. Three-month initial course for successful candidate. Apply Ministry of Education.

RADIO PRODUCERS. Applications are invited for posts as trainee radio producers. Candidates should have good educational qualifications and, in addition, imaginative ability. In view of the large number of applications expected, candidates should mention any activites they have taken part in which could be relevant to the work of a radio producer (dramatic societies, school magazine, etc.). Apply National Broadcasting Corporation.

SCHOLARSHIPS. The Ministry of Education is willing to grant ten special scholarships of four years' duration for students who will first work for a year in a state enterprise, chiefly as labourers and clerks. Subject to suitability, they will then take a university or technical college course which will enable them to return to their original place of work in a senior capacity. Good School Certificate essential.

SECRETARIES. Intelligent girls required to train as secretaries. Must obtain School Certificate this year. Girls from commercial schools preferred, but others may apply. Six months' basic training given by the Company. Apply Personnel Manager, Panafco Ltd.

TEACHERS. Applications are invited for places at a new Advanced Teacher Training College. Those accepted will follow a four-year course and will then be required to teach under Ministry of Education conditions. There are no application forms but candidates should give full details of their school careers and state clearly why they wish to become teachers. Training will be free and students will receive a small monthly allowance. Apply Ministry of Education.

EXERCISE 126
You have noticed that a local bus service has become very inefficient in recent weeks. Buses are infrequent and sometimes three or four going to the same place arrive at the bus-stop at the same time. On other occasions buses with empty seats fail to stop for you. Write a letter to the General Manager of the Company complaining about the service.

EXERCISE 127
Write a letter to the Manager of a hotel requesting him to reserve a room for you for the nights of 20th and 21st of next month. Mention that you want the cheapest room available and specify which meals you will require. You enclose a deposit.

EXERCISE 128
Write a letter to the editor of a local newspaper suggesting the building of a road. Give your reasons for believing that the road is necessary. Suggest that the local residents present a petition demanding the road to the authorities concerned.

Write a reply to the following letter, which is addressed to you. Explain that
you cannot settle the bill at the moment but that you enclose a small sum and
will send monthly payments for the next three months to cover the total cost.

International Book Co. Ltd.,
27 Charing Cross Road,
London, W.C.1,
England.
15 July 19___

(Your name and address)
Dear Sir,

Eight months ago we sent you the books shown on the attached invoice. You
undertook to settle the bill within three months of receipt of the books, but we
have so far received no payment. We regret that unless we receive payment in
full or a satisfactory explanation within two weeks we shall be obliged to refer
the matter to your headmaster, who is acting as your guarantor.

Yours faithfully,
T. Jones
(Overseas Sales Manager)

11 Topics for Continuous Writing

Ten Hints on Writing

1 Before writing anything make a short plan of your entire composition, using any help given in the question.
2 Use only words and constructions with which you are very familiar.
3 Avoid flowery and pompous language. The best writers of English express themselves in simple and clear language.
4 Avoid abbreviations. The place for these is in notes.
5 Make your writing interesting by illustrating what you say with examples.
6 Do not begin writing a sentence until you know how it will continue and end.
7 Begin a paragraph for each new topic.
8 Pay close attention to mechanical skills — grammar, spelling and punctuation.
9 Do not switch tenses unless the sense requires you to.
10 Check your work thoroughly at least twice. This will necessitate allowing a few minutes at the end of the time allotted.

Topics for Practice

1. Write instructions on how to:

(a) light a fire.
(b) play any musical instrument.
(c) make a chair or table.
(d) drive animals to market.
(e) make tea or coffee.
(f) prepare a meal.

(g) bind a book.
(h) ride a bicycle.
(i) play football, volley-ball or tennis.
(j) bargain.
(k) swim.
(l) make a telephone call.
(m) treat a cut.
(n) do the long or high jump.
(o) play a gramophone record.
(p) wash clothes.
(q) repair a puncture.
(r) sow seeds.
(s) fish.

2. *One of My First Friends*

Write about one of the first friends you made. Describe how you met him or her, the family he or she came from, what he or she was like, why you chose him or her as your friend, some of the games you played together or adventures you shared. Say if you are still friends or if you have lost touch with one another.

3. *My Education So Far*

Write an account of your education so far, using the following as an outline: the schools I have been to, the subjects I have studied and their likely value to me later in my career and as a citizen, and what I have learnt about the world and my place in it.

4. *My Career in the Next Ten Years*

Describe what you hope will be your career in the next ten years and what you will have to do to achieve it. Give your reasons for wanting to follow this career. Mention any study you will have to do and examinations you will have to pass.

5. *My Family Life in the Next Ten Years*

What changes do you expect will take place in your family circumstances in the next ten years? Do you plan to live with your parents, live alone or marry? What sort of house or flat do you hope to have?

6. *An Educational Trip*

A wealthy man has offered to arrange a trip for all the members of your class at his expense. The only condition is that all go away to a part of the country where you can study a topic connected with one of your school subjects. You could, for example, visit a site of historic interest, some natural feature, a dam, or a power station. Write an outline of the proposed trip, describing exactly where you would travel to, how you would live, and the study you would undertake. Your aim is to convince the wealthy man that the trip would be worthwhile.

7. A Statement to the Police

Two policemen have taken you to a police station for questioning. You are accused of breaking into a shop last Saturday evening. You are not guilty, of course, but you resemble the thief and are therefore suspected.

You are asked to write a statement. In it you explain where you were and what you were doing between the hours of eight and twelve last Saturday evening. Give the names of the people you were with or who saw you and any other evidence that might help to prove your innocence.

8. Advice to New Pupils

The headmaster has asked you to write two pages of advice to pupils joining your school at the beginning of next school year. You should deal with such topics as: subjects to be studied, examinations, discipline, games, other extra-curricular activities, and prefects.

9. Plan for a School Club

You have decided that a new school club should be formed. (It may be for any purpose you choose — stamp-collecting, gardening, helping the local community, etc.)

A notice is posted announcing that a meeting of all those interested will take place. At the meeting you speak on the proposal to form the club and you deal with these points (among others): the need for and aim of the club, what the activities will be, frequency of meetings, the committee, subscriptions.

10. My School

A visitor from abroad has asked to be conducted round your school by a pupil and you have been chosen for this role. He has just had a talk with the headmaster in his office and your tour will begin from there.

Give an account of your tour of the school and what you talk about during it. Some of the questions the visitor will ask are: 'When can pupils use the school library?' 'Is there an assembly every day?' 'Do you find the laboratories are adequately equipped?' 'Do all pupils take art?' 'How many school football (volley-ball, etc.) teams are there?' 'How have they done lately?' 'What other games are played?' 'Is there a school magazine?' He will, of course, ask other questions suggested by your arrival in different parts of the school.   *163*

11. An Exhibition

Describe how you would arrange an exhibition to show some of the changes that have taken place in your country in the last one hundred years. What objects would you include in such an exhibition and why? Possible topics you might treat are: medicine, education, transport, farming, the capital city, government.

12. A Book Worth Reading

Borrow a non-fiction book and write an account of it to encourage your friends to read it. Choose a book on a subject you are genuinely interested in. Do not give a chapter by chapter account but briefly describe the contents. Say exactly why you think the book is worth reading.

13. A Biography (or Autobiography) I Have Read

Give an account of the life of the person the book is about — his childhood, career, and main achievements. State what you admire in his life and in what way he is an example to you.

14. Should Girls Have the Same Educational Opportunities as Boys?

Decide for or against and write a composition using either of the following sets of arguments as well as some arguments of your own:

For: 1. Women have proved themselves capable of doing most jobs.
2. Girls will later be responsible for bringing up families.
3. Educated husbands prefer educated wives.
4. Girls have the same native intelligence as boys.
5. Women make up 50 per cent of the population and to neglect their education is to neglect the education of 50 per cent of the nation.

Against: 1. Educating girls leads to a breakdown of tradition.
2. Money spent on girls' education is often wasted because they marry and stop working.
3. Educated women are more inclined to disobey their husbands than uneducated ones.
4. Since there is not enough money to educate everyone, boys should be given preference as they are more likely to make use of their education.

15. The Value of Sport

Write a composition on the value of sport, using some or all of the following points: sport develops physique, sport trains character, sport is a form of relaxation, sport encourages competition, sport is a subject at which students who are not very good in class can sometimes do well.

16. *Wasted Money*

Write an account of how money is often wasted. Forms of waste you may deal with are: smoking; drinking; gambling; luxuries; unnourishing food; useless films, magazines and books.

17. *English, an International Language*

Many people no longer think of English as a foreign language, but as an international one. Write a defence of this idea, using these points (and others you may think of):
   (a) English is now spoken in many countries other than England.
   (b) Much more knowledge is available in English than in most other languages.
   (c) Using English it is possible to communicate with people in many parts of the world.
   (d) English has been influenced by many other languages.

18. *Should the Home Language be the Language of Instruction in Secondary Schools?*

In some countries the home language is used as a medium of instruction in both elementary and secondary schools. Do you think that the home language should be used in your country?
Possible arguments for and against are:
Against: 1. Books are readily available in English.
   2. Several languages are spoken in my country.
   3. Many of my secondary teachers do not speak my language.
   4. Many secondary pupils go on to study at universities where English is the language of instruction.
   5. English brings us in contact with vast areas of the world.
   6. We can still study and respect our language.
   For: 1. Secondary pupils are not fluent in English and therefore their progress is slow.
   2. Books could easily be translated from English.
   3. Our own language is part of our culture and we should use it.
   4. Using English results in British and American influence.

19. *Rules for the School Library*

Imagine that you have been put in charge of the school library and asked to draw up a new set of rules. Write them out. They should cover:
(a) hours of opening;

(b) period of borrowing;

(c) behaviour in the library;

(d) use of magazines and newspapers;

(e) reference section;

(f) membership of the library committee;

(g) any other points you think important.

20. What My School Could Do to Help the Local Community

Write an article for your school magazine suggesting what members of your school could do to help the local community. Possible needs are: roads, latrines, instruction in hygiene. State how and when you think pupils might be organised to carry out such work.

21. A Talk to Villagers on Literacy

During the next school holiday you are to go to a remote village where a literacy campaign is about to start. All the villagers who are to be taught to read and write will ask you to address them on the value of literacy. Drawing on your own experience as far as possible, tell the villagers the advantages they will gain from being literate. They will want answers to such questions as: 'Why should we learn to read and write? We live very well without such knowledge.' 'What is the good of reading and writing to a farmer?' 'Does being literate mean that we won't have to work with our own hands any more?' 'How long will it take us to learn to read and write?' 'Why do we need to learn to read and write when we have a radio in the village?' 'Will we be paid for the time we spend in class?'

Write the speech you would give, based on these and other relevant questions.

22. What a Student Council Should Have the Power To Do

In some schools student councils advise the headmaster on rewards and punishments, running clubs and societies, sporting activities, raising money to help the local community, the timetable, and other aspects of school life. Do you think your school would benefit from the existence of such a council? Outline the way (including the above) that it might be of help.

23. Should School Examinations Be Abolished?

You may use any or all of the arguments from one set below in addition to your own arguments. Make the composition interesting by referring to your own experiences as often as possible:

    For: 1. Teachers give too much time to preparing students for examinations and not enough to educating them.

2. Many people are successful in life even though they have never passed an examination.
3. Some students do badly in examinations because they are nervous.
4. It is wrong to assess a student simply on the basis of work done in the few hours an examination lasts. Term work is more important than examinations.
5. Examinations encourage cheating.

Against: 1. Examinations are the only scientific means of judging a student's progress.
2. Without examinations there would be no means of judging all students in the same way.
3. Examinations encourage hard work.

24. If I Were Headmaster of My School . . .

Suggest ways in which you would improve your school if you were the headmaster. You might change the system of rewards and punishments, allow the students greater or less freedom, lengthen or shorten the working day, re-arrange the timetable, improve the library and science laboratories, and organise sporting activities and extra curricular activities in a different way.

25. Has Science Made Life Easier?

Decide for or against and write a composition using either of the following sets of arguments as well as some arguments of your own:

For: 1. Travel is now fast and comfortable.
2. Communications have been greatly improved by the telephone, telegram, radio and television.
3. Gas and electrical heating as well as air-conditioning make life easier in certain climates.
4. Food is better produced and distributed.
5. Medicine makes it possible to treat illnesses more effectively; surgery and X-rays also help.

Against: 1. Modern weapons have made wars more terrible than in the past.
2. There is a great deal of noise in the modern world.
3. The pace of modern life makes many people ill.
4. The result of scientific developments is that people are more materialistic and therefore less happy.

Appendix

Reference List of Irregular Verbs

If you are ever in doubt about the past simple or past participle of a verb, refer to this list.

Present Tense	Past Tense	Past Participle
am, are, is	was, were	been
bear	bore	borne
beat	beat	beaten
become	became	become
begin	began	begun
bend	bent	bent
bereave	bereaved	bereaved
bet	bet	bet
bind	bound	bound
bite	bit	bitten
bleed	bled	bled
bless	blessed	blessed
blow	blew	blown
break	broke	broken
breed	bred	bred
bring	brought	brought
broadcast	broadcast	broadcast
build	built	built
burn	burnt, -ed	burnt, -ed
burst	burst	burst
buy	bought	bought
cast	cast	cast
catch	caught	caught

choose	chose	chosen
cling	clung	clung
come	came	come
cost	cost	cost
creep	crept	crept
cut	cut	cut
deal	dealt	dealt
dig	dug	dug
do	did	done
draw	drew	drawn
dream	dreamt, -ed	dreamt, -ed
drink	drank	drunk
drive	drove	driven
eat	ate	eaten
fall	fell	fallen
feed	fed	fed
feel	felt	felt
fight	fought	fought
find	found	found
flee	fled	fled
fling	flung	flung
flow	flowed	flowed
fly	flew	flown
forbid	forbade	forbidden
forecast	forecast	forecast
forget	forgot	forgotten
forgive	forgave	forgiven
freeze	froze	frozen
get	got	got
give	gave	given
go	went	gone
grind	ground	ground
grow	grew	grown
hang	hung	hung
have	had	had
hear	heard	heard
heave	heaved	heaved
hew	hewed	hewn
hide	hid	hidden
hit	hit	hit
hold	held	held
hurt	hurt	hurt
keep	kept	kept

kneel	knelt, kneeled	knelt, kneeled
knit	knitted	knitted
know	knew	known
lay	laid	laid
lead	led	led
lean	leant, -ed	leant, -ed
leap	leapt, -ed	leapt, -ed
learn	learnt, -ed	learnt, -ed
leave	left	left
lend	lent	lent
let	let	let
lie	lay	lain
light	lit, lighted	lit, lighted
lose	lost	lost
make	made	made
mean	meant	meant
meet	met	met
mistake	mistook	mistaken
mow	mowed	mown
pass	passed*	passed
pay	paid	paid
put	put	put
read	read	read
rid	rid	rid
ride	rode	ridden
ring	rang	rung
rise	rose	risen
run	ran	run
saw	sawed	sawn
say	said	said
see	saw	seen
seek	sought	sought
sell	sold	sold
send	sent	sent
set	set	set
sew	sewed	sewn
shake	shook	shaken
shed	shed	shed
shine	shone	shone
shoot	shot	shot
show	showed	shown

* Not irregular, but confusing as *past* is an adjective.

171

shrink	shrank	shrunk
shut	shut	shut
sing	sang	sung
sink	sank	sunk
sit	sat	sat
slay	slew	slain
sleep	slept	slept
slide	slid	slid
sling	slung	slung
slink	slunk	slunk
slit	slit	slit
smell	smelt, smelled	smelt, smelled
sow	sowed	sown
speak	spoke	spoken
speed	sped	sped
spell	spelt, spelled	spelt, spelled
spend	spent	spent
spill	spilt, spilled	spilt, spilled
spin	spun	spun
spit	spat	spat
split	split	split
spread	spread	spread
spring	sprang	sprung
stand	stood	stood
steal	stole	stolen
stick	stuck	stuck
sting	stung	stung
stink	stank	stunk
stride	strode	stridden
strike	struck	struck
string	strung	strung
strive	strove	striven
swear	swore	sworn
sweep	swept	swept
swell	swelled	swollen
swim	swam	swum
swing	swung	swung
take	took	taken
teach	taught	taught
tear	tore	torn
tell	told	told
think	thought	thought
thrive	thrived	thrived

throw	threw	thrown
thrust	thrust	thrust
tread	trod	trodden
undergo	underwent	undergone
understand	understood	understood
upset	upset	upset
wake	woke	woken
wear	wore	worn
weave	wove, weaved	woven, weaved
wed	wedded	wedded
weep	wept	wept
wet	wet, wetted	wet, wetted
win	won	won
wind	wound	wound
withdraw	withdrew	withdrawn
withhold	withheld	withheld
withstand	withstood	withstood
wring	wrung	wrung
write	wrote	written

Index